BUILD A BETTER YOU —STARTING NOW!

BUILD A BETTER YOU —STARTING NOW!
8

JOE LARSON
CHERON WAGEMAKER
RICHARD P. CORCORAN
BILL PICKERING, Ph.D.
ROGER HIMES
GINI GRAHAM SCOTT, Ph.D.
ARTHUR C. MOKAROW, Ph.D.
HARRY E. GUNN, Ph.D.
PHILLIP S. WEXLER
VIRGINIA LEE
KATHLEEN L. HAWKINS, M.A.
MICHAEL SIMONEK
JACK CLARKE, Ph.D.
ALAN G. ZUKERMAN, Ph.D.

DONALD M. DIBLE, Series Editor
CAROL FOREMAN BROCKFIELD, Senior Staff Editor

SHOWCASE PUBLISHING COMPANY
Fairfield, California

Library of Congress Catalog No. 79-63064
ISBN 0-88205-207-1

Printed in the United States of America.

Showcase Publishing Company
3422 Astoria Circle
Fairfield, California 94533

Distributed to the retail trade by
Elsevier-Dutton, Inc., New York

First Printing

TABLE OF CONTENTS

PREFACE

Hello. We at the Showcase Publishing Company are truly delighted to be able to bring you this eighth volume in our series *Build a Better You—Starting Now!* I'd like to use this opportunity to tell you just a little bit about this volume, this series, and our publishing company.

First, a word about this volume. Here you have the opportunity to benefit from the motivating, inspiring, and enthusiasm-generating ideas of 14 of North America's most exciting platform personalities—speakers whose messages are heard in person or on cassette by hundreds of thousands of people every year. Now you have the opportunity to read transcripts of their most popular talks and share their most carefully thought-out ideas and discoveries as they commit their observations to the printed page. These messages are now available for the first time in book form. *Build a Better You—Starting Now! Volume 8* is that book—the eighth in a planned series of 26 volumes.

Next, a word about this series. A full year of motivational, inspirational, and self-help "vitamins"—that's the idea behind this 14-chapters-per-volume, 26-volume series. That's a full year's supply of mental nourishment to be consumed at the rate of one chapter per day for 365 days. (Volume 26 will contain 15 chapters, for a total of 365 chapters.)

Drawing from the best of the tens of thousands of established and fast-rising stars in the self-help speaking field, this series is dedicated to bringing to wider-and-wider audiences throughout the world a vital message: *You can build a better you—starting now!* If you are truly dedicated, you can make it happen.

Finally, a word about the Showcase Publishing Company. Showcase was launched by the founders of The Entrepreneur Press, a nine-year-old company dedicated to publishing books for new and small business owners. (One of our titles, *Up Your OWN Organization!—A Handbook on How to Start and Finance a New Business,* has sold more than 100,000 copies.) All of the customers of The Entrepreneur Press are interested in self-help information. However, as we came to appreciate that a far larger audience existed for self-help information directed at personal development, the decision was made to start a new company dedicated to serving this larger audience.

As a public speaker myself (I regularly present more than 100 seminars a year), and as a member of several associations of public speakers, I realized that my fellow speakers could provide an enormous amount of material for the new audience we had chosen to serve. It was at this point that we decided to start Showcase. We sincerely hope you will agree that we did the right thing.

DONALD M. DIBLE
Publisher and Series Editor
SHOWCASE PUBLISHING COMPANY
3422 Astoria Circle
Fairfield, California 94533

BUILD A BETTER YOU —STARTING NOW!

JOE LARSON

While other kids dreamed of what they would be when they grew up, Joe Larson was busy launching his sales career. And after thirty years of "on the road" service, the eyes of this successful Sparta, Wisconsin, business executive and platform speaker still glow with the eagerness and excitement of the small-town boy.

The National Speakers Association recognized him for both hats he wears when they named him president in 1977-78. Currently its treasurer, he reaffirms his philosophy of "being involved." Larson views his three decades of public speaking not only as an opportunity to expand the influence of his company, but also as a way to motivate young people on their way up and increase the insight of those who have already "arrived."

A veteran of the door-to-door Fuller Brush and Jewel Tea circuits, Larson acquired the slumbering Sparta Brush Company in 1949. Through personal enthusiasm, vigor, and know-how, he nourished it into a leading international manufacturer of brushes for the dairy- and food-service industries.

Along the way he found that just tending the shop isn't enough. Admittedly hooked on people since boyhood, Larson has gained national prominence for his ability to control, motivate, and inspire a wide variety of audiences. Hundreds of national, state, and regional trade associations and fraternal organizations name him first choice as a keynote speaker at conventions, seminars, sales meetings, award banquets, and commemorative dinners.

Larson has often been referred to as the Herb Shriner of the food and dairy industries, but his listeners have more than jokes to take home with them. Larson comes across as a man full of positive thoughts.

A director of the Association of National Food Equipment Manufacturers and past president of the Dairy and Food Industries Supply Association, Larson is also a corporate member of the Rochester Methodist Hospital at the Mayo Clinic.

A leader in Wisconsin state and local civic affairs, he is a director of the Sparta Union National Bank and Trust Company and serves on the Board of Directors of the Wisconsin Association of Manufacturers and Commerce. He has been county chairman of a major political party, past president of the Sparta Chamber of Commerce, and has served as mayor of Sparta, Wisconsin.

Joe Larson may be contacted at Sparta Brush Co., Inc., 402 South Black River Street, Sparta, WI 54656. Telephone (608) 269-2151.

COMMON SENSE AND PLAIN DEALING

by JOE LARSON

Nothing astonishes men so much as
common sense and plain dealing.
—Ralph Waldo Emerson

Emerson said that way back in the 19th century. Sometimes I'm surprised to discover how many things we've forgotten about—ideas that worked well for a long time but aren't used any more just because they're old. Maybe we've simply gotten tired of hearing about them.

It's true that a few simple principles that were good fifty years ago will still be good a hundred years from now, and it could be that the application of some good old-fashioned common sense to today's business world could contribute as much as a heap of management courses from the best business schools.

I've never turned my back on good old common sense; I've been leaning on and learning from the examples of other people's common sense since I was a kid growing up in a small town in west-central Wisconsin. Back in those days, when households had iceboxes instead of electric refrigerators, there was an ice company in our town. The icehouse was located at the edge of the lake, and it was the custom to hold the annual ice harvest during the Christmas holidays so the schoolboys could help. Men would be hired to cut the ice, and young lads would be paid to crawl around inside the icehouse, packing sawdust between the big ice cakes. There would usually be eight or ten young fellows carrying heavy bushel baskets of sawdust back under those low beams and tucking it in around the ice. I was one of them. It was very hard work.

After my first morning on the job I walked home across the lake and told my mother, "I just can't do it. My back is killing me."

My mother didn't say a word. She fed me some lunch and let me lie down a few minutes. Then she took me by the ear, marched me over to the top of the hill and said "You get back there!"

Well, I went back, and to my surprise, that afternoon was a snap! I had gotten my second wind.

I had also learned a basic lesson in life. Had my mother let me give up that day, I wouldn't have known the pride or the satisfaction of success. I put a lot of stock in past experience, out of necessity and out of choice.

●

I was not able to finish high-school. I was a dropout before the word was even coined. My mother had been widowed back in the '30s, and in those days a widow's pension didn't go very far. Completing high-school became a luxury we couldn't afford.

4

Thus, I was very young when I realized that nothing would come easy, and that if I wanted something I was going to have to work for it. I had to develop the self-discipline to get up in the morning and put in a full day's work. It never occurred to me to feel bad about not being able to go on in school, and I attribute this to my mother's good old-fashioned common sense.

My mother used to tell me about a young neighbor whose husband wanted to do nothing but go to school. He took course after course, stopping now and then to teach somewhere for a year or two before moving on to study at yet another school. His wife worked to support him in a dozen different towns.

One day they came to call on my mother, who was then in her sixties. She was out working in her garden, and she tried unsuccessfully to get this young fellow to help her. As she told me later, "Why, he's been going to school all his life, and he doesn't even know how to hold a hoe!"

That pointed out another lesson for me. Knowledge isn't of any use if you can't apply it. A lot of people blessed with a formal education are unable to apply their knowledge once they've left the academic halls. That's a tragic waste of good, qualified people.

You can't expect to accomplish something in life by simply conjuring up a list of goals. You have to have a mind that isn't lazy and a back to match, so that when an opportunity presents itself you'll be prepared to take advantage of it.

●

I've often been asked if my success might not be due to mere luck. I used to wonder about that: Is there some force that plucks certain people out of the ordinary course of events and directs them instead toward worthwhile accomplishments?

5

Certainly some people believe in fate. Not I. I believe that a person who has worked hard and accumulated all the necessary information *is ready to take advantage* of opportunity. I believe that there will be a crossing of paths—the right chance at the right time—and the fellow who has done his homework *will recognize the opportunity and act.*

These paths of opportunity meet many times in our lives. But many of us fail to recognize them when we stand right at the intersection.

Looking back on my life I can see where I took advantage of opportunities as they came along. I was in the right place at the right time, and, more important, I *acted* at the right time. I was early blessed with a sense of my life's direction. While most boys my age were dreaming of growing up to be aviators, I saw myself as a businessman. Furthermore, I was already gaining experience—I was always trying to sell something, whether it was newspapers, Watkins products, or baby chicks.

I was drawn into business because it was fun for me. I like to talk. I was a natural-born storyteller. Speech was my favorite class in high-school. And when company came to visit I monopolized the conversation until my mother sent me off to bed.

Liking people and enjoying good talk made me a natural-born salesman. And every successful businessman must first be a salesman, for it is *he* who really sells the stuff: A company president must *sell the employees* on the product, and on the idea that if they produce, and produce well, everyone benefits—the customers, the company, and the workers. Everyone in the plant, right on down the line, must be sold *before* the selling job extends to the salespeople who distribute the product.

Another gift of great importance to me is an appreciation of humor. I believe that the Lord gave us humor for the same reason that the automobile manufacturers in Detroit put shock absorbers under a car and foam rubber in the seat cushions.

There's great value in not being too thin-skinned or too quick to take offense. It's been said that humor is the best way for people to keep their problems from overwhelming them. Turning the bright light of wit on a problem lessens the hold it has on us and makes it seem small enough to overcome.

I also think it's helpful to be able to picture yourself in a particular role, to know what is expected of you, and most important, to recognize what you expect of yourself.

I remember the heavy financial responsibility I had when I was still a boy. My father's long illness had made it necessary to take out a mortgage on our house. By today's standards it was a small mortgage, $800 at five percent interest. But every year we had to get that $40 together to pay the interest. (I still remember walking up to the big house on the hill with that money clutched in my hand.)

The year I had earned that interest money myself by picking apples—I was thirteen or so—we learned that my sister needed an operation. Those were the days before health insurance, and her husband had no alternative but to borrow the money from us. He promised to repay us before the mortgage payment was due, but as the deadline approached I began to imagine those people coming down from the hill and taking our house away from us. But the money arrived, just on the day it was due.

That traumatic wait taught me another valuable lesson. It strengthened my natural inclination toward optimism and reminded me that there is an inner peace that comes with knowing you've done your best. It heralded my basic business philosophy:

*Nobody has ever made a success out of security;
there are times when one must take a chance.*

•

That philosophy stood me in good stead in 1939, when I
was eighteen and working for the Works Progress Admin-
istration. I was part of a crew sent out to hunt the hills for
barberry bushes, the host plant for the rust that was damaging the local grain crop. I wasn't too happy doing that,
but it meant income of $39 a month.

A fellow was allowed to pick up other work if he
could. So in my spare time I sold baby chicks to the far-
mers who lived along those roads.

At the same time we had a roomer at our house, a
student at the local teachers' college who was a Fuller
Brush man on the side. The National Guard and the
Army Reserves were activated that year, and he was one
of those called up. Before he left he convinced me that I
should take over his Fuller Brush territory.

I remember going down to the post office where
the fellows were met by the WPA truck each morning.
When I told them that I was quitting to go out selling
Fuller brushes they just roared. They thought I was out of
my mind to give up the security of $39 a month in order
to do something that had never before made anyone a
success.

But for me it was the crossroad, the time for action
based on the experience I had. Their laughter made me all
the more determined to dare to be different. My defiance
carried me through the first two weeks, when I had to do
all my selling on foot.

At that time I was averaging about $100 a week. That
gave me enough confidence to march down to the car
dealer and announce that I had to have a car. Since I had
no money, I offered to leave my shotgun as collateral.

They wouldn't accept the shotgun, but they did give me a Model A for $75. Six months later I traded it in for a '37 Ford.

My district included Minnesota and Wisconsin. I won so many sales awards in my area that my boss came to me and said, "Joe, we're going to ask you a favor. We'll give you a prize, but we're going to take you out of the contest. Everybody says that there's no use in trying because Larson wins 'em all, anyway."

•

I think my success then came from the fact that I was developing the good business habit of always looking for a better way to do things. Accordingly, when the opportunity arose I took a two-week sales course with the Jewel Tea Company, although Fuller Brush persuaded me to return to work for them.

Shortly afterward, the country began to mobilize for war in earnest. I left sales work to help construct a nearby Army camp. Married, with a family, I was still ineligible for the draft.

And once again the formula of training plus timing presented itself. The very day the Army construction job closed, a friend employed by Jewel Tea Company mentioned that they were looking for an area salesman. I referred to the two-week training course I had completed, and I was hired on the spot. There I stayed until the Selective Service sent me my official "Greetings."

During my experiences on the road I learned some basic concepts that have helped me ever since. I learned that I had to make so many calls a day and that I had to always be on time. The women to whom I sold wanted to be able to set their clocks by me, and if I got behind not only was my schedule thrown off, but I was thought to be undependable.

I learned that if you are to sell quality you must *believe* in quality, that if you attempt to economize with cheaper service in just one little corner of your business, it's bound to show sooner or later.

My attention to dependability and quality service paid well, for when I returned home from the Air Corps, Jewel Tea Company had a job waiting for me. There then occurred another remarkable example of training and timing in my business life. A local shopkeeper suggested that I look into a line of men's footwear which promised a good future in sales. I arranged for an interview, took the necessary tests, and was told that I soon would be hearing from the company.

Two months later, on a Saturday morning, they called to say that I could start work immediately. But they were just twenty-four hours too late. The previous afternoon I had bought the Sparta Brush Company!

•

Everyone thought I was out of my mind to buy that rundown company. But I was encouraged by the business factors that I had come to rely upon and I was blessed with the optimism of a fellow not yet turned thirty: I could dare to be different. I knew I had the self-discipline to work hard, and I had a history of experience in the field. I saw it as the crossing of two paths—the right chance at the right time. I recognized that it was the time to seize the opportunity and to act.

I saw promise in the little dairy brush factory, run until then by a couple of nice old folks. I was not discouraged by the fact that it had been in the path of a disastrous flood, that what bristles were left had been damaged by water, and that the machinery was pretty well shot.

My wife Esther nearly suffered a nervous breakdown

at the thought of my leaving a secure job for such a gamble, but with her help we persevered. The first two or three years were a real trial. We did a lot of experimenting. We were determined to achieve and preserve quality. I was on the road from Monday through Friday, and I worked in the factory on Saturday and Sunday.

After selling direct we began to realize that if we were to grow we would need a nationwide jobber distribution arrangement. We realized, too, that we would have to establish some basic principles, so that our customers would recognize and appreciate that we would not sell direct.

We developed a written creed called "We Believe," in which we clearly established the roles to be followed by us, the manufacturer, and by our right arm—the reputable jobber. We acknowledged our responsibility to create products of consistently high quality, and we recognized the need for the jobber to supply his customers the service and counseling necessary for excellence in our product's performance. Some of our jobbers still have that creed hanging on their walls.

We developed a two-way display of trust which enabled both factory and jobber to excel in service. We supported our jobbers with vigorous trade-paper advertising and promotion and sales aids. We listened to their suggestions.

And we saw further that if we were going to serve the best interests of the dairy industry—once more hearkening back to the lesson I had learned as a boy—we were going to have to pay our share of the rent. We were going to have to be active in the industry's associations.

We joined.

•

Back in 1952 we were probably one of the smallest companies in the industry to join the Dairy and Food Industries Supply Association. The cost of the initiation fee and the first year's dues were so substantial that I had to borrow on my life insurance. (Nobody ever made a success out of security!)

Membership in the D.F.I.S.A. gave us the privilege of exhibiting in the big exposition. And I realized at those first large conventions that I wasn't going to learn anything by standing on the sidelines. I had to get acquainted with people.

I profited a great deal in those early years by listening to the older, successful people in the dairy industry. I went out of my way to ask them questions, and if I didn't get the right answers I concluded that I hadn't asked the right questions. It was an educational experience not available in books or in the classroom. I took all the information I could get back home with me, where I tried to adapt it to my own business.

It surprised me to discover that some members did not become involved. They were content to sit on the sidelines, asking why this or that had not happened, never realizing that it was because they had not volunteered to help.

In those early days I complained whenever I objected to something. That would result in my being appointed to a committee, where it was felt that I would be quiet! But with my love of conversation, I wound up as chairman, and was then elected a director. I went on to become president of the committee.

I was in awe the first time I sat at a board of directors' meeting. The average company represented on the board of the D.F.I.S.A. employed 400 or 500 people. Our little company had only 10 employees then. Most of the board members were products of prestigious eastern schools; many were presidents of dairy equipment companies that employed upwards of 2,000 people.

At that moment I got my second breath, the way I had that winter when my mother sent me back to the icehouse. It was then that I knew for certain that I could come from a background of limited education, take a small company with a good product and a good reputation, and, with the right kind of thinking and energetic exposure, accomplish the American dream.

•

Daring to be different has become a kind of slogan for me and for our company.

A couple of years ago my son Jack and I visualized a machine that would greatly improve the quality and the production of a particular type of brush. We traveled to Germany to meet with the designers and were told that no such machine existed. We replied that we were convinced such a machine was possible, and that the only reason one had not been built before was that no one had had the conviction to order an unproven $100,000 machine.

That machine took a year-and-a-half to construct. It is now successfully in use and performing beyond our expectations, and we have the satisfaction of knowing that it will take another year-and-a-half for any competitor to catch up with us. (Nobody has ever made a success out of security!)

I am reminded of a poem written by a friend and neighbor of mine from Scottsdale, Arizona. She, too, has never been satisfied with mediocrity. Neither age nor failing health has dimmed her spirit or lessened her appreciation of life. She wrote this poem about the subject of achievement:

> Ten men reach a canyon;
> Nine will hesitate;

But one will build a simple bridge
To bear his body's weight.

The land ahead is shadowy,
Obscure, as in a dream.
Nine men see the darkness:
One man sees a gleam.

He summons up his courage,
He subjugates his fear,
As, by himself, he mounts the bridge
To face a new frontier.

And so he crosses over
To alien lands unknown.
Uncertainties assail him as he
Stands there all alone.

His body says, "Stop dreaming!
Go back from whence you came!"
His spirit says, "Don't listen,"
And sets the bridge aflame.

—Eleanor Neissl

•

Editor's Note: In July 1980, fire destroyed the Sparta Brush Company plant and warehouse in Sparta, Wisconsin, causing a loss of more than one million dollars. Two months later the factory was back in nearly full production.

Larson cites Sparta Brush employees' cooperation and dedicated efforts, along with community support, for turning a business disaster into "an opportunity to act," confirming his conviction that "It's not important what happens to a fellow—it's how he responds that really counts."

CHERON WAGEMAKER

Consultant and lecturer Cheron Wagemaker has worked with people from all walks of life, including government, politics, private industry, homemaking, and business. She has trained housewives, children, executives, and professionals. Her courses and speaking topics span many facets of self-improvement, as her main interest is to help individuals build their lives in every area, from nutrition and physical fitness, to assertion and positive living.

Cheron helps people utilize their own power and potential by bringing out the best they have to offer. She helps them make changes to create a more harmonious life.

Cheron grew up and attended college in Tallahassee, Florida. While employed by the Office of former Florida

Governor Reubin Askew she was instrumental in developing the Governor's Council on Physical Fitness, which is still expanding to help many Floridians.

Cheron became interested in assertiveness training and positive living techniques because she wanted to improve the quality of her own life. The techniques she learned have worked for her in both her personal and professional associations.

In addition to lecturing and teaching her own courses she has trained many others to be instructors and lecturers. Since she began teaching assertiveness training, positive living, and related subjects, Cheron has appeared on radio and television and has been featured in newspapers including the *Pensacola News Journal,* the *Gainesville Sun,* and the New Orleans *Times Picayune.* She is a member of the American Society for Training and Development and is an educational consultant for Batten, Batten, Hudson & Swab, a human resources and development company.

Cheron Wagemaker can be contacted by writing c/o Batten, Batten, Hudson & Swab, 2711 E. Coast Highway, Corona Del Mar, CA 92625; telephone (714) 675-4340.

FACE THE ISSUES

GUIDELINES
FOR ASSERTIVE BEHAVIOR

by CHERON WAGEMAKER

I would like to give you a clear understanding of the differences between assertiveness, non-assertiveness, and aggressiveness and help you identify your typical behavior pattern. Then I will offer some techniques for becoming more assertive.

Why is there a need for assertiveness articles, books and training? Many individuals are not aware that they have the right to be treated with respect, to be listened to, to express their opinions and desires as if they really matter, and to say *no* without feeling guilty.

Every person has the right to be who and what he is without apologizing or holding back, but many people need a little outside assistance. They need help in raising their self-esteem so that they can understand assertive behavior and practice it consistently. That is why organized assertiveness awareness and training came about. The majority of this training has been geared toward women because of a past widespread belief by many women that it is their lot to always play the passive role. However, this article is written for both sexes. Many men also need to understand and develop assertive skills.

I learned about assertiveness by trial and error many years before I began reading about it in books. I learned that in order to develop assertive behavior you have to be willing to look honestly at yourself. Above all you have to want to change your old programming.

I am sure you have times, as I have, when everything in your life seems to be running smoothly. Then along comes something unexpected to upset the apple cart and challenge everything you have inside. That's when I take time out to look at myself, identify bad habits, and make a plan of action to change them.

I hope that reading this chapter will give you help in smoothing out life's bumpy path. Perhaps an assessment of your assertiveness behavior will provide the insight that turns the light on: May you have many lights of wisdom turn on in your life.

How Did I Get This Way?

Before we discuss the characteristics of the three types of behavior, especially before you begin identifying and trying to change your habit patterns, it's important to understand their origins. We are taught by our environment, primarily in our first seven years. (Some say life moves in seven-year cycles and others say twelve-year cycles; I won't argue with either view. The point is that early childhood has a profound effect on your personality and your habits. You learned much of your present behavior from the people who raised you.)

When you were young you learned how to manipulate and argue just like the adults around you. You also learned positive habits like showing concern, love, and affection for others; standing up for your rights; and pursuing what you want in life. As an adult you have your own personality, hopes, dreams, and life purpose. However, all of this is colored by the habits and attitudes you learned as a child.

These habits and attitudes are powerful. They permeate every area of your life. If you were taught the old classic, "Children should be seen and not heard," guess what happened the first time you were required to address a meeting? That old programming played back in your mind and made you freeze.

Or maybe you were taught that you were incompetent: "Keep your mouth shut, dummy!" Or, "Oh, let me do it. Can't you do anything right?"

Or superior: "Don't hang around with them—they're not as good as we are."

Maybe you were taught to avoid conflict: "Don't make waves," "Always be a perfect lady (or gentleman)," and "Remember, you catch more flies with honey than with vinegar!"

The list is endless; the effect is the same—we're all programmed for future responses.

The subconscious mind is like a computer. It makes no judgments on what is fed into it. It does not label things positive or negative, but merely acts out what it receives. Therefore it's up to you as an individual to reprogram your own computer the way you want it. Knowing where you picked up an undesirable attitude is part of the battle of changing it, and it will require a sincere effort on your part.

How do you know if assertiveness is an area you

need to polish and practice? The person who is shy, afraid to speak up, and reluctant to say *no* when he or she wants to is often painfully aware of needing improvement. Other people who have been outgoing, loud, and boisterous all their lives may be unaware that they are in reality aggressive, with detrimental consequences to themselves and others.

To give you an idea of the three types of behavior, here is a typical problem. A co-worker without a car frequently asks you for a ride home. You don't want to continue driving this person because it takes you out of your way. Here are three responses you could make.

- *Non-assertive.* "Well, OK, I guess I can drop you off." (Afraid of the other person's reaction.)

- *Aggressive.* "Look, if I dropped everyone off who asked me, I'd be running a taxi service every week. Isn't it about time you got a car and quit bothering everyone all the time?" (Lashing out.)

- *Assertive.* "I understand that you don't have a car, and I gladly helped you when I was able to in the past. However, my schedule won't allow me to continue giving you rides. Why don't you contact the personnel office and arrange to get into a carpool?" (Direct and unapologetic. Goes the extra mile of offering a possible solution.)

Am I Non-Assertive?

Everyone has some degree of non-assertiveness and some degree of aggressiveness.

Let's look at non-assertive behavior for a few moments. It isn't always easy to deal with life's challenges. Non-assertiveness means refusing to face issues. It means avoiding your true feelings and running away from conflict at every opportunity.

Certainly some situations should be avoided, just as others need to be dealt with. But the non-assertive person has difficulty making the distinction. Non-assertive people let others make their decisions for them. They are passive and submissive to the degree that they are not in control of their lives.

You can tell when you are using non-assertive behavior because it is usually accompanied by anger and resentment. Some signs of non-assertiveness could be sweaty palms, rapid heartbeat, averting your eyes, nervous laughter, slouching, and overall dissatisfaction.

All too often the non-assertive person has been playing out the same dramas over and over for years, keeping all his feelings bottled up inside, where they continually build. When some of those feelings finally escape, maybe in lashing out at a friend, spouse, or co-worker, they are hostile and aggressive. Periodic outbursts of this sort indicate non-assertive behavior.

It's easy to blame others for why our lives don't work. (If it weren't for my wife, husband, boss, children, poor health, lack of money, or heavy workload—you name it!) But after years of getting what you want through dishonesty, indirectness, and manipulation, the burden becomes too great to handle. Non-assertive behavior results in very little peace of mind and a lot of ambiguity.

Here are some questions to help you determine if you have been living your life in a non-assertive manner.

- Do you frequently use the word *should?*

- Do you feel resentment toward someone (lover, boss, relative, spouse, or friend)?

- Do you vent your feelings through explosive anger rather than calm discussions?

- Do you constantly procrastinate?

- Do you feel shy and quiet around people you don't know (especially those in a different financial or social bracket)?

- Are you generally afraid of saying *no* because you worry about hurting someone or fear what he or she will think of you?

- Are you always the nice guy trying to please others?

- When someone is trying to take advantage of you, do you go along rather than speak up?

- Do you let others make decisions for you?

- Do you blame other people if things don't go well?

- Do you let others make you feel guilty?

- Will you do *anything* to avoid conflict?

- Do you expect other people to know what you want and get angry if they don't come across?

If you answered *yes* to the majority of these questions, keep reading—this chapter is definitely for you!

Am I Aggressive?

There is common confusion between assertive and aggressive behavior. Many people equate assertiveness with aggressiveness. The confusion may spring from the dictionary, which may give *aggressive* as a synonym for *assertive*, and vice-versa. Webster's defines *aggressive* as, first, "inclined to start fights or quarrels"; second, as "ready or willing to take issue or engage in direct action, militant"; and third, as "full of enterprise and initiative, bold and active."

It's not unusual to hear the word *aggressive* used in this context: "He's very aggressive. In our business we need a person like that to get the job done." Here, the second meaning would apply.

However, if an enterprising person chose to use combative, militant behavior to get the job done—running over people, failing to communicate, and forcing issues to the point of causing injury or extreme discord, the results would be negative. Generally when we talk about aggressive behavior, and always in psychological usage, it is in this negative sense.

Some people were raised to be aggressive. They were taught as children to bully, threaten, yell, and walk over people—to do anything to get what they wanted. We commonly refer to these people as bossy and domineering. Rarely do they experience a relaxed or satisfying relationship of any kind. They are too busy trying to prove their points and maintain their control over others.

Overly aggressive people don't have enough faith in themselves to open up to the genuine give-and-take of honest communication. Instead they shout, stomp, and threaten themselves into ulcers or worse. Their behavior inevitably takes its toll on their bodies. To borrow from the wise words of "Desiderata": *Speak the truth quietly and clearly . . . avoid loud and aggressive persons; they are vexations to the spirit.*

Often non-assertiveness leads to aggressive behavior. A person can be taught to be overly adaptive and accommodating so that he or she is unable to deal with conflict when it occurs. Often the things that upset this person are not the same things that trigger an argument. For instance, John comes home every day for two weeks and snaps at his wife. He blames her for trivial things such as lack of toothpaste in the bathroom, misplacing his checkbook, and having to go to a dinner party for which they both accepted the invitation. John storms around the house making unreasonable demands and accusations and has closed off all real feelings and communication.

What upset John was being passed over for a promotion at work. He knew he had earned it. He deserved it, but when he was informed that he had not gotten it he held in his anger and neglected to present the facts that might have made a difference. So now John's non-assertiveness has surfaced at home in aggressive tendencies and in issues unrelated to the real conflict.

The cultural conditioning that teaches women to be docile and men to be *macho* has caused many assertiveness problems. Today, when women speak out assertively at home or on their jobs after many years of being quiet, they are often labeled *aggressive*. However, it is normal and natural for all of us, men and women, to assert ourselves. We all have the same basic hopes and desires for love, fulfillment and financial security. And although our training and programming often stands in our way, society is gradually changing. Both men and women can be strong assertive individuals who decide what they want in life with mutual respect for one another's rights and desires.

Here is a list of questions to help you pinpoint your aggressive behavior patterns:

- Are you always the authoritarian in your personal and business relationships?

- Do you always demand your way and take responsibility from others, rather than share it?

- Do you often stand with hands on hips and feet wide apart?

- Do you frequently point your finger or fist at others, using the blaming word *you,* while telling them what they did wrong or why they are wrong?

- Do you pound your fists on the table to demand support or to get your point across?

- Do you frequently act superior to others?

- Do you blame, accuse, or label without bothering to get the facts?

- Are you considered by others to be more curt and rude than polite?

- Do you always have to win?

If you answered *yes* to the majority of these questions it's time for some honest self-searching and analysis.

It helps to read self-help books and take a few self-improvement courses. There is a wide choice of courses that are well respected and can help you become aware of the areas you need to work on. Courses on such subjects as assertiveness, self-awareness, goal-setting, time management, stress reduction, motivation, and meditation all contribute in some way to your overall well-being and make communication with yourself and others much easier. I have found them to be well worth the money invested.

If you can tell from what you have read so far that out-of-balance aggressiveness is one of the areas you need to correct, it could be that you have been attempting to overcompensate. Sometimes this is caused by fear that the other person will not listen to what you are trying to say. Try relaxing. Take three deep breaths and ask yourself, "What's happening here? Do I really have to put my point across in this manner? Am I jeopardizing my own self-respect and the respect of others by doing so?"

Realize that no matter who is right or wrong, your viewpoint is *equally as important as the other person's.* And so are your self-composure and self-esteem. Check whether the subject you are arguing, shouting, or making demands over is really the main issue of concern. If not, be honest with yourself and get down to the basics of what is really going on.

Am I Assertive?

Being assertive means being yourself and communicating your true feelings, wants, and needs in a direct, honest, and unapologetic manner. It also means making your own choices in life and taking responsibility for them.

All the assertive people I have ever known have had a secret quality—self-love. I don't mean that they think the world will not turn without them. I mean that they genuinely like themselves and accept all aspects of themselves as being perfect and whole, even the parts they are still polishing.

It's true that underneath your own rough edges are sparkling diamonds. But if you've been putting yourself down in any area of your life, this may be hard for you to accept. To quote from "Desiderata" again: *Be yourself. . . . You are a child of the universe, no less than the trees and the stars; you have a right to be here. And whether or not it is clear to you, no doubt the universe is unfolding as it should.*

Some people think that if a person talks about self-love, he or she is being "selfish." Divide that word and you get *self-ish* or *of the self.*

Jesus taught "Love thy neighbor as thyself." To me

that doesn't mean either loving others more than myself or leaving myself out and becoming a martyr; and it doesn't mean loving others less than myself. Jesus said *as thyself,* and to me this means that my neighbor and I are equal, but that I have to love myself first because I cannot give out what I don't have inside.

When you love yourself, you're good to yourself and others as a matter of course. You do the best you can to express your wants, needs, and opinions in every situation. You neither walk over others for what you want nor do you allow others to walk over you. The *inner you,* which in many people remains masked and hidden throughout their lives, becomes the *outer you*—so there is no hidden conflict. What goes on inside is consistent with what you say and do on the outside.

People respect and respond positively to a well-balanced person who says what he means and means what he says. They tend to feel comfortable with an assertive person. Even if they don't agree with that person's viewpoint, they know they can depend on his directness and steadfastness. It may be great to have people like you, but it is far more important to have them *respect* you!

Assertive people don't like game-playing, manipulative ploys, or double talk. They are courteous but they don't mince words. You can identify many or all of the following behaviors as characteristics of assertive people:

- Respects and likes self.
- Maintains a positive attitude.
- Shakes hands firmly. (This shows that the person has a good grasp on his life.)
- Laughs frequently and has a good sense of humor. (This person plays the game of life rather than letting it play him.)
- Speaks clearly without hesitation.

- Stands straight and walks briskly.
- Instigates conversations and helps people talk about themselves.
- Is of genuine service to others without becoming a do-gooder or getting "burned out."
- Demonstrates leadership and creativity.
- Has a rewarding home life and lasting personal relationships.
- Handles problems as soon as they arise.
- Can interview for a job or give a speech without emotional distress.

How Can I Change?

If you think you may be handicapped by non-assertive or aggressive behavior and want to do something about it, you have several options. Of course the best course of action would be to enroll in an assertiveness class. There you will be able to interact with others and practice your new behavior patterns in a nurturing environment. However, if no classes are available to you, you can begin working on your own. Start today with these guidelines.

1. RELAX

- Sit in a comfortable position.

- Take three deep breaths and hold each for a few seconds before exhaling.

- Tell every muscle and organ in your body to be calm and relaxed, starting at the top of your head and working down to your feet.

- Clear your mind of anxieties and task-related thoughts.

- Picture yourself at the beach or some other enjoyable place.

2. REVIEW

- Consider how you were taught to handle conflict as a child, particularly how your parents handled conflict. If your mother sulked and threw the dog out the back door and your father shouted, you may have a tendency to handle conflict in similar ways.

- Were your parents able to communicate their feelings, wants, and needs? If so you stand a chance of being able to do the same on a consistent basis.

- Were you taught to use any possible tactics to get your way? Or were you taught always to comply?

3. SEE THE CHANGE

- Visualize yourself as you want to be. See yourself saying things in a new way. See yourself saying all the things you want to say but have held inside.

- Decide what change you desire in yourself and write it as a goal.

- Discuss it with a close friend or your spouse, and ask for comments and feedback.

4. MAKE A DECISION

- Imagine the worst thing that could happen if you took action or decided against action in a given situation. (Things rarely turn out as bad as we imagine they will. It's our doubts and fears that produce the greatest anxiety.)

- Make notes on what you're going to say or do and how (positively and calmly).

- Practice going through the situation both mentally and physically.

- Make notes on how you felt and how well you conducted yourself, so you can improve next time.

5. USE BODY LANGUAGE

- Look directly at the person you are talking with. Don't avoid meeting the other person's eyes.

- Stand or sit in an erect, relaxed manner.

6. WATCH HOW YOU SAY IT

- Speak calmly and clearly from your diaphragm.

- Be direct and unapologetic. (Remember that it's the tone of your voice that people will notice most.)

- Never attack anyone directly: "You make me angry!" Instead, refer to their action or lack of action in a given situation: "I'm angry about the things you said to me at the party."

Remember that the brilliant minds that shaped history never attained greatness by holding back and fearing the consequences.

Don't expect to totally overhaul your habit patterns overnight. You've been practicing your habits diligently for years. Have patience with yourself and be understanding.

Never equate your performance with your self-worth. Regardless of how many times you may try something and fail, with hard work and determination you eventually will succeed. I wish you happiness and success, and again, from "Desiderata": *Be yourself.* ... *Whatever your labors and aspirations, in the noisy confusion of life keep peace with your soul. With all its sham, drudgery and broken dreams, it is still a beautiful world. Be careful. Strive to be happy.*

RICHARD P. CORCORAN

Richard P. Corcoran has delivered hundreds of speeches to schools, church groups, civic groups, service organizations, conventions, and conferences in the United States and Canada. He covers such topics as psychological implications of disability, problems of the blind, rehabilitation of the handicapped, and spiritual values. He is recognized as an authority on parliamentary procedure and has served as parliamentarian for many local, state, regional, and national organizations.

Dick was born and raised in Ottawa, Illinois, where he completed his elementary and high-school education. He lost his sight when he was completing high-school, and subsequently enrolled in an adjustment training program for the blind.

In 1953 Dick was graduated from Loyola University with a Bachelor of Science in Humanities. He was then employed as a sales representative for three years, during which time he received a Salesman of the Month award.

In 1959 Dick moved to North Dakota to organize and implement a program of services for the blind and visually impaired. It was the first such program for the Department of Vocational Rehabilitation in the state.

In 1965 he received his Master's degree in Education with special emphasis on rehabilitation problems of the blind from Western Michigan University. As a rehabilitation counselor he continues his work with people of various disabilities. In 1972 he was honored with a national award, Elkins Counselor of the Year, in San Juan, Puerto Rico.

Dick has also received the Distinguished Toastmaster, the highest award given by Toastmasters International, and the Outstanding Handicapped Citizen of North Dakota award. He is a member of the National Association of Parliamentarians.

You may contact Dick Corcoran by writing to 1805 Linda Drive, Mandan, ND 58554; or telephone (701) 663-8708.

YOU'VE GOTTA WANT

by RICHARD P. CORCORAN

Have you ever wondered whether you would accomplish anything in your life? Have there been times when you asked yourself, "Will I ever achieve success?"

First as a visually handicapped person, and later as a blind person, I was perplexed and discouraged by that question. I doubted myself and my ability to succeed.

Now that I have attained some degree of success, I often wonder how I did it. What was the predominant factor in my success? Was it some trait of character or personality? Was it the knowledge gained along the way? Was it my faith and self-confidence? These were all important, but I see that the primary reason for my success was my *overwhelming desire* for it. It was very important for me to do something meaningful with my life.

A person can establish realistic and worthwhile goals but lose sight of them by not wanting them badly enough. A person can develop great self-confidence and faith in the future, but without a burning desire to obtain results these qualities will not be used to good advantage. To achieve success a person has *gotta want* success more than anything else in the world!

We grow our own success from a field of desire which is generously planted with seeds given to us by our Heavenly Father. The five seeds which I have found to be of greatest benefit to me are those of trust, hope, self-confidence, faith, and enthusiasm.

Trust

We are born completely lacking in trust, and the first year of life is spent in developing it. Our parents nurture it with loving care as they stroke, hold, bathe, and feed us. As we learn trust we begin to crawl, to stand alone, and to walk tall. In succeeding stages, as we experience individuality and begin to make choices, trust continues to be an issue. So long as we grow we continue to move emotionally from lack of trust toward increased trust.

The trust learned in infancy must expand until it becomes a part of us. Trust is what enables us to listen and learn from those around us, for if we are suspicious of others we cannot hope to learn from them. And it is our teachers, friends, and co-workers who provide many of the nutrients that make us grow.

As a blind person, I had many lessons to learn in trust. By virtue of the fact that I became more dependent on other people for assistance, I could not have made satisfactory adjustment to my loss of vision without some trust in others. I still do have to trust sighted people for help in such areas as getting directions, reading printed material, operating certain machines, driving, and selecting articles to purchase. Through the need to be involved with others I have developed many meaningful friendships and relationships, and they have enriched my life immensely.

One lesson I have learned is to always check with a second person when asking directions. People often give incorrect directions.

I'll never forget the time I was traveling to Cleveland, Ohio, to attend a Toastmasters International Convention. As luck would have it, dense fog forced us to land in a city a hundred miles away. I took a taxi to the bus station, where I hurriedly asked the ticket agent about transportation to Cleveland. He sold me a ticket and told me to rush out to the loading gate because the bus was leaving in a matter of minutes.

I asked someone for help, grabbed his arm at the elbow, and followed him to the gate. There I was quite perplexed to learn that there were three buses on the verge of pulling out.

I took a chance and boarded the first bus. Soon after I discovered that all the other passengers were patients from the state mental hospital. The bus driver began counting the passengers so as to keep track of them. "One, two, three, four . . ."

Coming to me, he asked "Where are you headed?"

I told him I was going to Cleveland to the annual convention of Toastmasters International. "In fact," I said, "I'm scheduled to speak at the noon luncheon, and Toastmasters is paying me $500."

The driver looked at me and went on counting: "Five, six, seven . . ."

How many of you remember the story of the man who walked across Niagara Falls on a tightrope? No one believed he could do it, but as they watched, nonbelievers became believers.

The man said "Next week I'll walk across pushing a wheelbarrow," and he successfully completed this feat, too.

Then he announced that he was ready to walk across the falls *pushing someone in the wheelbarrow*. He asked for a volunteer: "Who will ride in the wheelbarrow?"

The believers drew back. They had suddenly become non-believers again. Only one young girl came forward. She told the man "I'll ride in the wheelbarrow," and she did. She was his daughter.

Now that is real trust! That is the extent to which you must be open to trust—trust in yourself, trust in others, and trust in a higher power. (Have you ever known anyone woefully lacking in trust? Such a person is not even able to enjoy life.)

Another dimension of trust is the relationships it enables us to develop. Relationships cannot exist without trust. And without relationships, our lives would be empty. We all need love and closeness to a special somebody in our lives.

Hope

Without hope we cannot begin to tackle the task before us. We have to be able to dream of victory, and we need hope to dare to dream.

My seed of hope was nourished in a way I could never have foreseen in imagining my future. It was during my junior year in high-school that my ophthalmologist gently broke the news to me. There was nothing that medical science could do to stop the progressive degeneration of the retina in both of my eyes. He suggested that I learn Braille and prepare myself for some field in which I could work successfully as a blind person.

My mother cried. I accepted the verdict with passive

resignation: "Certainly this must be the will of God."

I became extremely appreciative of my partial vision. It allowed me to finish high-school, but by then I was no longer able to read printed material. As a consequence, many jobs were denied me.

For several years I lived as a recluse, with little social contact outside my immediate family. But even then I still had a strong desire to make something out of my life, to become a success. What I was lacking was the means—the skills, the confidence, and a plan.

Nearly four years after that day in the ophthalmologist's office, a key figure entered my life. A rehabilitation teacher from the State Services for the Blind in Illinois offered to teach me Braille. His inspiration and instruction nurtured my seed of hope.

A few years later the same teacher offered me an opportunity to enroll in a six-month rehabilitation-adjustment training course for the blind and visually impaired. I accepted this opportunity even though the course was to be held in Chicago, miles away from my home.

Why did I leave my safe comfortable home—where I knew I would always be cared for—to strike out on my own in an unknown city? My rehabilitation teacher had led me to realize that there was indeed a possibility that I could earn a living and do something purposeful with my life. Now that I had hope, my desire to succeed burned ever brighter.

You will always encounter problems and difficulties when you try to turn your dreams into successes. But growth results from problems, and difficulties add interest and excitement to life.

You are probably familiar with the accomplishments of Demosthenes, one of the world's greatest orators. Born with weak lungs and a speech impediment, Demosthenes was ridiculed and scorned. Yet he had a driving ambition to become a lawyer and plead cases in court. He was determined to overcome his speech handicap. To accomplish that he practiced speaking with pebbles in his mouth. To strengthen his lungs and vocal cords, he walked along the seashore, shouting above the waves when they were their noisiest. Through determination and perseverance, Demosthenes achieved his goals and turned his problems into accomplishments.

Self-Confidence

Confidence is what you need most to succeed. It is inextricably tied up with self-image, and more than anything else, the image you have of yourself determines what you learn, what you read, what career you choose, what life partner you select, and what attitude you develop. Your self-image is the core of your personality, and strong self-image is built on confidence.

A public school teacher told me about a class discussion she led on self-image. She said to her students, "Today we are going to talk about your identity. Do you know what that means? Your identity is who you really are inside. Do you know who you are?"

A young boy stood up and said, "My name is John Jones. I know I am black and I know I am beautiful, because God don't make junk." Now that's confidence!

Certainly the experience and training I received at the adjustment training program for the blind increased my self-confidence and taught me the need to develop it further. I'll never forget the first time in my life that I traveled home alone at night.

Although I still retained some daylight vision, from early childhood I had been totally blind at night. I had never traveled alone at night at home, much less in a strange city. On this occasion I was careful to learn every significant landmark along the way, and especially the intersection where I would change buses, from the friend who accompanied me into the city.

The real challenge began as I started my solo trip back home. I was nervous and apprehensive. I constantly asked the bus driver where we were, because I was afraid of going beyond my stop. I worried about finding myself in a completely unknown part of the city, especially one where mugging was routine.

In spite of my fears I got off at the right stop, and I made the right bus connection. The second bus driver also let me off at the correct street. Then I had to align myself with the curb, cross the street, and walk that long, long block to my house.

How relieved I was when my cane hit the familiar steel grating in the sidewalk near my home! How happy I was to find the particular chain fence that told me I was in the right spot! That was a night of triumph, a night of victory. For the first time in my life I had traveled alone at night!

That trip was the first of many more that were to follow in my lifetime. It helped me to take a giant step in self-confidence and it also taught me the value of trusting others. Later I found myself traveling unaided throughout the city of Chicago.

I must admit that my travel experiences were not all positive ones. An example of what could go wrong was the time I went to Mobile, Alabama, on my first trip to the deep South. In the rush of making trip preparations I had not eaten any breakfast or lunch, and by the time I reached Mobile I was very hungry.

Someone guided me to the hotel desk, and a bellhop took me up to my room. But then he left me all alone. I had to have a meal, so I tried to find my way back down the unfamiliar corridor to the elevator. I made it that far, and there I met someone who helped me to the restaurant.

The restaurant was crowded and the hostess led me all the way to the back to an empty table. I waited some four or five minutes before I heard the sound of footsteps coming my way. A waitress set a glass of water on my table, and just as quickly hurried away. After some time I heard her footsteps again, and she laid a menu on the table and vanished before I could say a word.

I was going to make sure that I caught her attention the next time. The third time I heard those familiar footsteps, the waitress came to my table and asked what I wished to order.

I quickly said "Miss, I can't read this menu. Will you please tell me what the selections are?"

She came back with an indignant reply: "Suh! What makes you think I can read any better than you?"

Another experience which taught me self-confidence was completing undergraduate studies at Loyola University. University life was brand new and exciting to me. I had to make many adjustments, such as learning to live independently in a hotel near the campus, reading printed materials and assignments with the help of a sighted reader, and orienting myself to the buildings and classrooms on campus. With the mastery of each new task, each new course, and each new extracurricular involvement, I experienced personal growth. With each success I became better able to tackle new experiences. And each new experience became part of my success.

Faith

You must have faith to achieve success—faith in yourself, faith in your ideas, and faith in the accomplishment of what you are doing. Loss of faith causes loss of dreams.

During World War II, when the American occupational forces arrived at a small Polish town, they found the villagers to be tired, weary, and desolate. The townspeople demonstrated no desire to rebuild their town or to go on living. They had lost all hope.

When these people were asked what they needed most, they replied, "The restoration of our church bell."

An old man explained it: "We get up in the morning and we go to bed at night by the bell. A baby is born and a man dies; it is told by the bell."

More than they needed food to eat and clothes to wear, the people of that town needed their church bell. To them the bell was a symbol of something lasting, something they could depend upon and live by. It was a symbol of faith.

The bell was restored, and only then could the villagers begin to rebuild their town, and, even more important, their own lives.

We all need a symbol of faith, a reliable source of strength. We cannot depend entirely upon ourselves—no one person can stand alone and reach the top. We all need the power of faith in God. Do not place your faith on a cupboard shelf—when you come back you may find it gone! Carry your faith with you and live by it.

I did not always have the faith that I have today. During my last few months at Loyola University I was overcome by doubts and fears. I lacked faith in the future. I was depressed by the reality of needing to obtain employment, and by my seemingly dim prospects. By that time my loss of vision was complete.

I finally accepted a position as sales representative for an internationally known encyclopedia firm. I worked for that firm for three years. I even realized some degree of success, as I once won the "Salesman of the Month" award. In spite of this, I was realizing no personal satisfaction in my work.

Although I could see no future for me in that type of employment, I continued in that job. Like most people, I refused to listen to the message I was receiving. I put in several more years of long hours and poor eating habits, until my deteriorating health forced me to give up that line of work.

Then I spent eight months in a sanatorium with pulmonary tuberculosis. During my stay there I had more than enough time to meditate on life and its meaning, and it was there that my seed of faith was nurtured and flourished. God's healing power was in clear evidence as I steadily regained my health. I had to admit that he was the source of all strength in my life. In him I found the assurance that my future plans would be fulfilled.

Some men possess the kind of faith they need right at the beginning of their dreams. Such a man lives in Bismarck, North Dakota. As a young lad, this man developed a window-cleaning product in his own basement and then worked long hours selling it door-to-door. He later produced it in larger quantities, started his own factory, and produced and sold other products. Today he owns and operates a multimillion-dollar business, the Gold Seal Company. He had an idea and he nourished it well with self-confidence and absolute faith.

The Bible assures us that believing without doubting will bring good results. So if you have a dream, have the faith to stay with it, no matter how big or frightening it may be.

Enthusiasm

We should wear enthusiasm as matter-of-factly as we wear our clothes. Enthusiasm springs from within and gives us new life. It turns on the bright light of our being; it makes our faces glow and our eyes sparkle. It provides us with a source of energy that never runs out.

In his book *Reach Out for a New Life*, Robert Schuller defines enthusiasm this way: "Enthusiasm is that mysterious something that turns an average person into an outstanding individual."

Dr. Schuller goes on to compare enthusiasm to a joyful fountain that bubbles and shouts to the world: "I can! It's possible! Let's go!"

I know a woman in Minot, North Dakota, who is the perfect example of enthusiasm. She suffers the multiple handicaps of total deafness, partial blindness, and Parkinson's disease, but she reads Braille for personal pleasure and uses a Tellatouch machine to communicate with sighted friends. She practiced and studied these communications skills all day long and far into the night. Confined to a wheelchair, she is seldom able to visit others outside, but when visitors call upon her she is now able to talk with them in her fashion. Her enthusiasm for learning to communicate brought great joy into her own life and the lives of others.

What is life without trust, hope, self-confidence, faith, and enthusiasm? Each of these is essential for success. Nurtured and cultivated in your garden of desire, they will join with the driving force within you—the yearning and craving, seeking and wanting, the nudging and pulling of your soul. *You gotta want*—and then those seeds will bear for you the fruit of success.

BILL PICKERING, Ph.D.

Bill Pickering was born in Florida and spent his early childhood in Dallas, Texas. He attended college at Taylor University in Upland, Indiana, and studied philosophy and theology at Emory University, Boston University, Andover Theological School, and Harvard. Later he changed to the field of psychology and completed his Ph.D. degree at the California School of Professional Psychology, Los Angeles campus.

Bill took his internships at Los Angeles County-USC Medical Center and at the Pasadena Child Guidance Clinic. He has had wide clinical experience in the areas of hypnosis, child and adult psychotherapy, and treatment of alcoholism and psychosomatic disorders. In addition, he is a practicing industrial psychologist with a background in management consulting, stress management, career assessment, and communications. Bill presents seminars in stress management, communications, and voice improvement.

Bill's public speaking career began when he was twelve years old, and he spent his teen-age years as a boy evangelist. He is a well-traveled keynote speaker, toastmaster, and seminar leader, whose presentations are marked by information, inspiration, and humor.

Bill's own philosophy of speaking governs his method of communication. As he puts it, "I believe those who leave a seminar or keynote speech should be able to say 'I learned something today, I was inspired, and I smiled and laughed a little.'"

Bill is a member of the National Speakers Association, Toastmasters International, and the American Society of Clinical Hypnosis. He is in the private practice of clinical and industrial psychology in Orange County, and he is a clinical instructor in the Department of Psychiatry and Human Behavior, California College of Medicine, University of California, Irvine.

You can contact Bill Pickering by writing to 13792 Dall Lane, Santa Ana, CA 92705; or telephone (714) 832-2212.

HYPNOSIS: A HOUSE NOT MADE WITH HANDS

by BILL PICKERING, Ph.D.

It's a hot Friday afternoon and the traffic is heavy. You only hope to get home by 6:30 or 7. Most of the other drivers, like you, have their windows rolled up and their air conditioners turned on. You come to a complete stop at a red light, and as you glance around at the lone occupant of the vehicle on your right, you notice that she is moving her mouth and gesturing wildly. It's amusing to see someone talking to herself in such an animated way—but actually we *all* talk to ourselves! Each of us carries on an "inner dialogue."

The lady in the car was probably talking to herself about something that required a solution. She was preparing to make a decision and to act on that decision. This kind of inner dialogue plays a very important part in

the outcomes of all our lives. The messages we give ourselves make us what we are. It's the selling job we do on
ourselves that's responsible for our success or failure. As
John Milton wrote, "The mind is its own place, and in
itself can make a heaven of hell, a hell of heaven."

BUILDING THE INNER HOUSE

Each of us is "under construction"—we are always in-
complete. Part of the excitement and adventure of life is
to grow and to change. Our minds are such an integral
part of this process that our daily thoughts can build us
up or tear us down. In the broadest sense, we are all construction or demolition people. The house we are building inside of us is not made with our hands, but with our
thoughts, our feelings, and our daily behavior. Through
the messages we give ourselves—our inner communication—our "inner house" is being fashioned and shaped
every moment of every day.

One very useful technique for convincing ourselves
of our own abilities and potential is self-hypnosis. You
may think you have never been in a trance. But can you
recall the last time you drove for one or two hundred
miles over a flat ribbon of road, maybe in Texas or Arizona? Do you remember being bored with the unchanging
vista of grass, tumbleweeds, and asphalt? Then, all of a
sudden, did you "wake up" with the realization that you
had passed through several towns without being fully
aware of them? This is called "highway hypnosis," and
you were certainly "under," no matter what label you
choose to put on it.

The phenomenon called hypnosis is a state of consciousness separate from either unconsciousness or
sleep. Hypnosis is *not* mind control; during hypnosis you
are in control of your own mind. It is virtually impossible

to force a person to violate his ethical and moral value system in a hypnotic state; he will come out of it and resist.

Hypnosis *is* an altered state of consciousness; it is one bridge to the unconscious, and, among other things, it's a way of opening up the storehouse of forgotten memories, dreams, and guiding lights (or darknesses) that have helped to shape your personality, behavior, and emotional responses. It is helpful in changing or reprogramming your personality.

Hypnosis can be used for both positive and negative outcomes. It can make you sick or make you well. It's such a powerful force that research is now being done on the application of hypnosis in curing cancer.

A Few Cautions

I've been using hypnosis for many years in clinical and industrial psychology, and I've found it to be a valuable tool in bringing about positive changes in human beings. Ninety percent of the people who come into my office are capable of hypnotizing themselves, although they may not realize that they have really been "under."

Before going on to specific self-hypnosis techniques, it is important to point out precautionary measures. Generally speaking, self-hypnosis is a safe procedure. It is certainly less hazardous, in most cases, than chemical change agents taken by mouth or by injection. However, it is wise to understand what you are doing before you induce a trance. Be sure that you know exactly how to bring yourself "out." (A tried-and-true method is to count backward to go under and forward to come out.)

I advise waiting a few minutes after a hypnotic experience to re-orient yourself before getting behind the wheel of a car or doing anything else which requires alert concentration.

If you are currently under a doctor's care for some serious ailment (such as a heart condition), I advise you to consult your physician before engaging in self-hypnosis.

You can probably avoid any potential problem by making an appointment with a qualified psychologist or psychiatrist for a one-hour orientation in self-hypnosis. Call your county psychological association or psychiatric association. (If you are referred to someone by a friend, ask the hypnotist if he or she is a member of the American Society of Clinical Hypnosis; this society admits only qualified psychologists, psychiatrists, or dentists to membership.)

Inducing the Trance

There are many ways to induce hypnosis, and I'm going to suggest two of these. Basic to each is *concentration*. Before you begin, find solitude. Sit in a room alone, eliminate distractions, and look inside yourself. Turn off any thoughts other than what you are about to do.

When you are ready to begin, select an object you can see well—a clock, a picture, a lamp, or a spot on the ceiling—and focus your attention on it. Say the following words, either aloud or to yourself. (When you are learning this skill, you might find it more helpful to say the words aloud.)

If your object is an open fireplace, say: "I'm concentrating on the fire in the fireplace. I'm looking neither to the right nor to the left. As I look more and more intently, my eyelids will gradually flicker; they will become heavier and heavier over my eyes. When they are ready to close down over my eyes, I shall allow them to do so. My eyelids are flickering more and more now; they are blinking more and more rapidly; they will close down over my eyes very soon."

Keep repeating these words (repetition is very important in hypnosis) and then say: "When my eyelids do close down over my eyes, I shall go deeper into hypnosis by counting backward from five to one."

As you count backward, say *deeper* with each number: "*Five*, I'm going deeper; *four*, deeper still; *three*, still deeper."

An Alternate Method

Sit in a relaxed position and close your eyes. Now think of some beautiful place you have been, such as a vacation spot or a childhood home. Picture every detail of that happy and peaceful scene, using all your senses.

Recall the colors of each object inside and outside the place. Think of the smells. "Feel" the textures. Listen to the sounds—voices, birdcalls, waterfalls, farm machinery, kitchen implements.

As you concentrate on this scene, attempt to feel as if you are there again. Then, after several minutes, say to yourself: "As I think about seeing, touching, tasting, smelling, and hearing, I am going to go deeper and deeper." By the time you have reached some depth in hypnosis, you will be ready to proceed with the other suggestions I am going to give you.

Tips to Help You

You can do just about anything under hypnosis that you can do in a normal conscious state. You can talk, walk around, whistle, sing, and even open your eyes. But I suggest that at first you remain silent with your eyes closed. This will insure maximum concentration.

Learning hypnosis is something like learning to play a musical instrument. It takes practice, and you have to become accustomed to it. After your first venture you may say: "Oh, that wasn't anything. I wasn't really hypnotized. It was just like meditation or concentrated reading." But the more you get over your unrealistic expectations of what hypnosis *should* be, the more the hypnosis experience will become real to you.

Don't be discouraged if you don't live up to all of your ideas about hypnosis. Don't worry about what you've heard about hypnosis on television or from other people. Most of that is probably inaccurate. As you hypnotize yourself, you will find your own way in your own time.

Deepening

This is an optional second step. If you have worked with either of the two induction methods and want to go still deeper, you may find this second phase helpful. Deepening is a technique that intensifies your concentration and leaves your unconscious mind with a more indelible imprint.

One deepening technique is to imagine yourself on a descending escalator. Perhaps you have already used the numbers five to one. Here you use *floors* five to one. As the escalator moves down, say: "*Floor five,* I am going deeper; *floor four,* I am going deeper; *floor three,* I am going still deeper; *floor two,* I am going still deeper." When you reach floor one, say: "I am stepping off the escalator; I am on the first floor."

You may prefer to think of floating along on a large rubber raft, or even a magic carpet. See the numbers as you pass by. Watch the numbers go by and say: "I'm going deeper and deeper as I pass each number. *Five,* I am going deeper; *four,* I am going deeper . . ."

WORKING ON PERSONAL CHANGE

At this point, I'm going to suggest several options for change. You may choose to use any or none of them in order to fit the "cure" to the patient and find the method that works best for you. Remember that these options are for use after you have completed the induction procedure.

Option One

I suggest that you use the deepening method with this particular option. What I'm going to ask you to do now is to put on rose-colored glasses and go back in time. Tell yourself: "I'm going to be wearing rose-colored glasses throughout this experience. I'll look only at the *positive* things that have happened to me—the things that were uplifting, inspiring, and joyful." (If you're one of those rare people who says "I can't recall anything good about my past," I do not recommend this option.)

You may want to use a calendar and tear off the pages as you go backward, or if you are an H. G. Wells fan, you may imagine yourself in a "time machine." Another idea is to count your age backward, beginning with your present year. Whatever, it's important to have some focal point to concentrate on.

As you go back through time, you may decide on an arbitrary stopping place; let's say it's age four. Decide you will go back in time to age four.

Count back to age four and begin reviewing the *positive* experiences stored in your mind. Allow your senses to see, hear, smell, touch, and taste each remembrance. Move forward in time from there, in whatever vehicle you have chosen for your journey, remembering as you go.

When you are ready to come out of your time exploration, say something like this: "I am now going to move forward to the age I was before I began this journey through time. I will use my [calendar, time machine, magic carpet, set of numbers, etc.] to bring me to my present age. When I reach my present age I will be in my *regular* waking state. I will remember all these inspiring and positive experiences from my former days. I will feel relaxed and refreshed, and renewed in body and mind."

When you reach your present age say: "I am now fully alert, and I will open my eyes and be still." (The reason for sitting still or lying still is to give your mind and body an opportunity to re-orient themselves after a period of detachment and total relaxation.)

Option Two

After you have put yourself into a trance or relaxed state, choose some special problem you are working on—let's say you want to change your self-image.

When you are "under," picture yourself going through the steps leading to a successful self-image. If you are in sales, for instance, picture yourself making several phone calls or house calls. To simulate reality as closely as possible, think of *no,* as well as *yes,* answers. Recall one of your better days, and build a "scene" under hypnosis. Think of the discouragements, difficulties, and setbacks, as well as the sales you actually closed.

When you're ready to come out of your hypnotic exercise, tell yourself: "I'm going to use this successful sales day as a springboard for other days. I'm going to feel encouraged in my body and my mind, and this is going to propel me toward more successful living and more profitable selling."

Then count forward: "*One,* I'm coming out of my other state of consciousness; *two,* I'm feeling refreshed and inspired; *three,* I'm moving toward my regular conscious state; *four,* I'm feeling encouraged and wider awake; *five,* I'm almost fully roused; *six,* I am fully roused and in my regular waking state. I will open my eyes and sit [stand, lie] still."

Option Three

You may be one of those people who say: "I've never had a successful sales day." If so, it may interest you to know that your mind is capable of *simulating* or *manufacturing* a successful sales day, complete with hard times and good times.

I have often helped patients to induce dreams in my office, and I have seen them create a positive experience, just as if it had really happened. In like manner, you can manufacture a successful sales day. Use real places and people as stage props to make your hypnotic experience convincing. Use your imagination—just as you did so often when you were a child. It makes no difference whether your hypnotic day was relived or made up— either way it can bring you future successes.

You can't argue with results!

A scene which you can look back on for inspiration is highly valuable and affects your body, as well as your mind. And if you experience one successful day as a consequence of your work under hypnosis, you then have a new source for successful sales.

One follow-up for this technique is to picture yourself receiving an award in front of several hundred people. Imagine every detail—the color of the plaque or cup, the "feel" of the metal, the sound of the presenter's voice, and the thunderous applause of the audience.

One objection often heard in connection with "manufacturing" a successful day under hypnosis is, "Suppose the person is disappointed with what he is able to create?"

Aren't people disappointed in or out of hypnosis? The primary point is to *anticipate* and *expect* the most optimistic outcome; this helps you to rise to the occasion, both mentally and physically.

These techniques can be adapted to your own line of work, whether you are a public speaker, a restaurant owner, an advertising executive, a politician, a housewife, a parent, a waiter, or a construction worker.

OUT-OF-TRANCE HYPNOTIC TECHNIQUES

There are many hidden rewards in hypnosis; one of them is that you sharpen your ability to tap into your unconscious—that infinite reservoir of power and motivation. As you practice concentration, you will find that you are able to do a lot of hypnotic work at your job, at lunch, or on coffee break. You can do some strong programming of that computer we call the mind while your eyes are wide open. Let's look at some of the ways you can use hypnosis "on the run."

Use a Verse

Select a saying, a Bible verse, or a line from a poem. Start the day by spending 15 or 20 minutes to induce a short trance, as suggested in the induction procedures. Put your verse into the unconscious part of your mind. You can use the same technique without trance by repeating the verse several times. It also helps to type or write it on a 3 × 5 card and look at it as you say it out loud. Take this card to work, and put it on your desk (or on the dashboard of your car if you travel from place to place).

Let's assume you have chosen a Bible verse, II Timothy 1:7.

God has not given us the spirit of fear,
but of power, *and* love *and a* sound mind.

I've indicated the key words. Repeat this verse, looking at the card, eight or ten times before going to work. Take the card with you and use your coffee breaks and lunch hour to review your source of inspiration.

If you're using a word for the day, such as *success*, say it aloud. Keep it in plain sight and look at it frequently during the day. Use it in a sentence; think of a scene that illustrates it; and picture yourself in that scene. Think of yourself in a situation where you are achieving success.

Use an Object or Symbol

Do you have some "lucky" object that you use like a "rabbit's foot"? Some people carry religious medals or sentimental objects. In every Roman Catholic church there is an icon of some sort—a representation of something supremely significant in that faith. Such objects are sensory reminders. They engage your senses to tap into your unconscious. When one sees, smells, or handles symbolic things, one is reminded of a personal heritage, a personal commitment, or a value system.

Anything can serve this purpose for you. For example, if you rummage around in your attic, you may find an old coin that was given to you by your grandfather. Perhaps you still remember what he said at the time, and maybe it even served as a lodestar for your life. If that were true, each time you pulled out the coin you would be reminded of your grandfather and the wisdom he shared with you.

You can derive the highest benefit from a symbolic object if you handle it often during the course of each day. Look at it, review the associations or sentiments connected with it, and use it for your hypnotic good.

Use a Color

Make up your own color chart; that will be more effective than using any existing color system. Write down what each color means to you. Here is an example, just for illustration.

- RED—power, inspiration, life, fire
- YELLOW—adventure, expansion, risk, butterflies
- BLUE—warmth, intimacy, quiet, sky
- GREEN—renewal, expression, birth, plants, grass

Notice that the last word beside each of my colors is a natural phenomenon—fire, butterflies, sky, grass. These add to your description by appealing to your senses. You have *seen*, *felt*, or *smelled* fire, butterflies, sky, and grass. Make color cards by printing your associations for each color on a card of that color. You might also cut each card into a representational shape—such as a butterfly.

Look at each card several times each day, say the descriptive words, and think about the positive messages they hold for you.

Daydreams

Dreams are part of our very survival. It has been shown that our dreams at night affect our ability to make sense out of the events of the day. Daydreams are just as significant. Jerome Singer and other psychologists have done substantial research in this area.

When I was an elementary school student in Dallas my teacher invariably wrote on the back of my report card: "Daydreams—looks out window."

I still daydream and look out of the window, and my daydreaming contributes to the treasure-trove of ideas which make up my livelihood. My best thoughts come through daydreaming.

In my stress seminars I show executives, managers, and workers how to make their daydreams pay off in less tension, more efficient functioning, and clearer thinking. You can condense a great deal of time into a daydream. In a mere matter of minutes you can accomplish an hour's work. You can think through a problem, imagine numerous paths toward its solution, go down each path, and "see" the result. Most idea people I know are daydreamers. They are sometimes laughed at, ridiculed, and dismissed as idle speculators. Yet daydreaming is a form of work, particularly when daydreams lead to momentous decisions. Daydreaming is part of the process of bringing an idea from seed to full flower.

THE POWER OF HYPNOSIS

You may say to yourself: "I've been using some of these techniques for a long time without hypnosis. I don't see how hypnosis will make them any more effective."

Hypnosis is valuable because it is a *strong bridge to the unconscious.* The unconscious mind is often difficult to reach. This powerful repository of images, dreams, words, events, and motivational forces is inaccessible through usual channels of communication.

My professional training included several years of psychoanalysis. I learned later that I could have accomplished the same amount of personality change in half the time through hypnosis! I think of hypnosis as a kind of "pipeline" to the unconscious. Even though hypnosis is a conscious state, it is closer to the unconscious than our customary waking condition. For this reason, the techniques I have outlined can be doubled or tripled in effectiveness when you add hypnosis.

One demonstration of the strength of these hypnotic tools was seen in a film shown at one professional society meeting. It follows a rhinoplasty operation that was performed from start to finish without the use of anesthesia. The patient relied completely on hypnosis to deaden her pain.

The assistant surgeon was shocked (and was caught by the camera with his mouth open), as the surgeon scraped around some very sensitive areas of the patient's face. The patient had been talking to the surgeon with her eyes open since the work began, and half-way through the operation she said to the doctor, "Is there anything else I can do to help you?"

He replied, "Yes, you can stop hemorrhaging."

And the patient obliged—through the power of hypnosis, she stopped the bleeding.

I am the first to attest to the power of positive thinking, as I have used it successfully. But, I do not believe that positive thinking alone is strong enough to overcome some of the built-in pathology which has been planted, watered, and cultivated through years and years of negative thinking and feeling. In some instances, on the other hand, I have found hypnosis to be a near-miracle. It replaces worn-out attitudes with transplants for permanent change.

There are some things you just can't do for yourself. (I would never advise do-it-yourself dentistry!) But I do believe that hypnosis can be a useful self-applied tool to create ongoing progress toward your personal goals. These techniques for induction, deepening, and personal change will prove valuable as you adapt them to your own needs.

Here is a partial list of areas in which hypnosis commonly produces change:

- Increasing self-esteem
- Modifying personality and attitude
- Increasing focus for defining your goals
- Altering habits (smoking, weight control)
- Changing adversity into advantage
- Increasing the power of symbolism
- Bridging the gap between conscious and unconscious
- Sharpening your senses
- Visualizing your potential

Hypnosis, like any other tool, requires hard work and commitment to be effective. It will not serve as a panacea, and you will experience plateaus as well as progress.

Hypnosis is like physical exercise; you may feel sore after using muscles which have been neglected for some time. Parts of your mind have been dormant for years; hypnosis will probe these forgotten corners of the brain and let you in for some surprises, shocks, and discoveries.

I contend that you have been hypnotizing yourself for years, for good or for ill. Why not make it pay off now in positive change?

ROGER HIMES

Roger Himes is an attorney-at-law in the Denver metropolitan area, where he lives with his wife Eileen, their daughters Lisa and Dawn, and their newly adopted son Ralph. He's an attorney who's more interested in developing people than in merely handling problems.

Roger is the author of three books, *Counselor, State Your Case!*, *No-Fault Marriage*, and *Searching for Reality*. He's a songwriter and composer with approximately 50 songs to his credit. He's just finished recording an inspirational and patriotic 45 rpm single of two of his original songs, "America!" and "This Is God's Country."

Roger is a speaker and seminar leader and member of the National Speakers Association. He conducts two seminars: "You, Inc., the Human Corporation," and

"No-Fault Marriage/No-Fault Divorce," and speaks on a variety of subjects. In addition, he's always willing to bring along his guitar. As Roger says, "Music often communicates where words sometimes fail."

When speaking of Roger, others say "His enthusiasm for life is contagious!"

You can reach Roger Himes by writing P.O. Box 21821, Denver, CO 80221; or telephone (303) 426-1770.

YOU CAN'T RUN KNEE-DEEP IN MUD!

by ROGER HIMES

An ancient proverb says, "For though a righteous man falls seven times, he rises again."

People don't drown by falling in the water, but by *staying* in the water. You're not a failure because you fall, but because *you refuse to get up!* You're not a failure because you fail, but because you consent to being a failure. It's a matter of attitude.

Fear of failure is something that haunts many people, and it's a crippling disease. It causes procrastination and inactivity. It discourages people from setting goals and striving for success. Many people are afraid to try again once they have failed. Others reason that if they don't have any goals, they can't fail to achieve them.

Yet it's really true that it's better to have tried and

failed than never to have tried at all. And you're not a failure until you reach the point of saying "Who pushed me?" or "I quit!"

Who Pushed Me?

We're a race of buck-passers! We tend to avoid reality by passing blame off onto others. We've learned that transferring the blame eases the *guilt* we feel inside. But this is like treating the ulcers without treating the cause of the ulcers; it doesn't deal with the root-cause of the ailment.

Most of us are masters of passing the buck in our marriages, and we let the bad habit carry over into other areas of our life as well. Many psychiatrists help us along. They try to ease their patients' guilt by blaming parents, siblings, friends, bosses, education, and environment. (Some theories of psychology even hold that it's easier for a person to live in a make-believe world than to face some of the pressures of reality!)

The only thing that blaming others does is to keep us from coming face-to-face with our own worst enemy and our single greatest problem: ourselves. We don't understand that accepting the blame for who we are and what we've become isn't self-condemnation. It's not damaging. Rather, it's the means by which we can be set free. It's a paradox that's difficult for us to understand.

Roger Himes is the only person in this world I can control. When I personally accept control of my life, instead of passing the blame for my life situation off on others, then I'm in the driver's seat and I'm off down the road of success.

I have to be willing to admit I'm wrong and that maybe I've blown it. Alcoholics Anonymous says we must first of all admit that we have a problem, and this is often the most difficult step. It's true, and it isn't limited to drinking. Admitting that I don't have it as together as I want everyone to believe, admitting that I'm a less than totally successful person, is to say that I'm at least a partial failure. And failure, in any form, is difficult to cope with.

If I pass the buck and say "Who pushed me?" then I'm blaming others. This may make me feel better temporarily, but it doesn't allow me to confront the culprit, who is me. Avoiding blame points me in the wrong direction. I'd like to share a few lines from a song I wrote:

We spend so many empty years
wishing upon stars,
It sometimes takes eternity
to see things as they are—
Not only as we wish they'd be
and not just from afar.
When we face reality
we discover who we are.

A failure is a person who continually says "Who pushed me?" A failure is a person who refuses to take responsibility for who he is and where he is. He's a failure because he views his deplorable situation as outside his control.

Remember that you can't pass the ball and dribble it at the same time. However, if the problem is *you,* then *you* can change any set of circumstances for the better.

I Quit!

We never know how many steps it takes to walk a mile until we've taken the last step. Quitters are losers because they never play the entire game. As soon as they get a little bruised, they sit out on the sidelines and watch.

If football players quit trying as soon as the other side scored a touchdown, the game would be dead. As it is, many good games are won in the last quarter of play.

I recently saw a bumper sticker that said "Patience is a virtue that carries a lot of *wait!*" Patience is something we all need. Human nature is designed with a shortage of patience. ("Lord, I want patience, and I want it *right now!*")

Yet patience is a strong characteristic of the success-motivated person. Endurance and perseverance function in the present tense—they're neither past nor future. And they should be a way of life rather than a sporadic gritting the teeth and bearing it. The words "I quit!" have no part in the successful person's vocabulary.

We all choose whether we're going to be winners or losers. Granted, a lot of things happen to us that we don't like, and many of them we can't prevent. But we all chose *how we're going to respond* to them. If we allow adverse circumstances to rule us, we'll remain defeated. Are you a ruler over your circumstances, or are you ruled by them? *What happens to you isn't half as important as how you respond to what happens to you.*

We're all faced with failure. We all experience failure in our jobs, in our relationships, in our health, in our marriages, and with our children. None of us is perfect and never will be. We can, however, grow progressively more and more successful in every area of our lives by making appropriate choices in our minds.

Sow a Thought

Proverbs 23:7 says, "As he thinketh in his heart, so is he." The human being is an inside-out process. Many people are *apparently* successful; few are truly successful. Many people never learn the secret that success is more *who you are* than what you do, and, especially, what you have.

"Sow a thought, reap an act; sow an act, reap a habit; sow a habit, reap a lifestyle." It's an inside-out process that begins in our heads.

If we're going to be successful, we must *know* what we mean by the term. The definition must encompass our entire lives, not just the present moment, and it must touch all areas of life. And most important, if we're striving toward success, we must, by definition, be free to fail.

Failure is perhaps one of the hardest words in the English language to define. By definition, it is a falling short of an anticipated goal or expectation (which must also be defined). Failure can't be defined in and of itself; it must be defined in conjunction with success. Without carefully planned goals, visions, and expectations, there can be no failure to reach what it is that's desired. Without a concise understanding of success, there can be no failure.

To most people, success is spelled *$ucce$$*. Now, there's nothing at all wrong with money. As a matter of fact, money is essential in our culture. Money isn't the root of all evil. It's our attitude toward money that causes us trouble; money itself is no more than a tool.

We've all heard at least one story about a millionaire who made it to the top of the financial world only to discover that money isn't the magical key to life. Many financially-successful people have broken families and delinquent children—products of the frantic climb to the top. If money is fulfillment, why are there so many suicides among the affluent? If this is success, who needs it?

On the other hand, countless people are content to drift through life being "just average." I don't know about you, but I don't care to be just average! The best definition of average I've seen is "where the best of the worst meets the worst of the best." That somehow doesn't seem too exciting.

The Total Reality

Success must be defined in terms of personal, vocational, physical, and family life; in terms of your relationships with yourself, with others, and with God. The human being is a three-part organism made up of spirit, soul, and body. Ignoring any area of ourselves is like trying to run on one leg—we are truly and severely limited.

Just as you can't be successful without defining what you mean by the term, you can't start really living until life has an essentially personal meaning for you.

It's one of the maxims of the positive mental attitude (PMA) teachings that a person is not truly ready to begin living until he's ready to die. First things must come first. We must deal with the ultimate life issues before we become bogged-down with the humdrum daily issues that constantly bombard us. Life can quickly become stale if all we deal with is day-by-day requirements.

Our refusal to deal with the reality of death is one thing that commonly gets us knee-deep in mud. Death is one reality that can't be disputed, and it affects us all. Yet most of us run from this fact throughout our lives. We don't confront it until we're *forced* to.

This amounts to a conspiracy against ourselves, and it winds up doing great harm. We bury thoughts of death deep within us, and we bury them alive, not dead. Therefore, they return again and again to haunt us. We'd be better off coming to grips with that ultimate goal early in life.

I have a favorite story about a jester and a king. The jester was so foolish that the king gave him a fool's staff and instructed him to carry it everywhere he went until he found someone more foolish than himself to give it to.

The jester kept the staff for many years. Then, when the king was on his deathbed, he called the jester to come and make him laugh. He told the jester he was going on a long journey and wasn't ever coming back, and that he didn't want to be sad in beginning such a long journey.

The jester asked what preparation the king had made for his long journey and the king replied that he had made none. At that point the jester took his fool's staff and presented it to the king. He had finally found someone more foolish than himself.

Most of us are mere jesters in life. We don't take life seriously—we've heard that life is a game. But that's a fallacious saying. Life isn't a game, but rather a very serious business. There are serious issues to consider and decisions of the most supreme consequence to be made.

As Henry Wadsworth Longfellow put it, what if the grave is not the goal? What if "dust thou art, to dust returnest," does not include the soul?

We are meant to come to grips with the total reality of life, and then to creatively make as much of it as we can. This is success in the fullest sense of the word. If you haven't personally come to grips with the reality of death, you're not putting first things first. You're majoring in minors, and you're still playing the game of the jester. Seek the Creator of Life, who alone has the keys to life and death.

The Eyes of Faith

Too often we have vision problems. Most of us are either nearsighted, farsighted, or downright blind. The person who hasn't come to grips with the issues of life is a blind person with no idea where he's going. What does life mean to him? Why is he here? He doesn't know, but moves around in a stupor, following anything he bumps into.

The nearsighted person usually sacrifices his future

for the present. All he can see is right now, and he's doing everything he can to live for this particular day, this particular moment. It's true that you should live each day of your life as though it were your last. You should give this day the full measure of all you have to give. But knowledge of the future is essential to do this.

Our life is like a parade—there's a beginning, a middle, and an end. We can't see into the future of the parade of our lives, but we can see into the future through the eyes of faith. We can't live in the future, but in order to be successful, we must know where we're going and when we plan to arrive.

Conversely, we can't be successful by being only farsighted. We can't live only for the future. Many of us have plans for great tomorrows while today remains a mystery. Yet today should be the least mysterious of all. Yesterday is a cancelled check, tomorrow is a promissory note, but today is cash—spend it! Spend it by putting first things first and setting your life's priorities.

If you have only future hopes, you'll die on the vine before your fruit ever ripens. Just as we need plans for the future, we need current, short-range goals to compensate for our nearsightedness. The truth of the matter is that we must learn to live our lives *in balance.*

His Own Masterpiece

A successful person is a dreamer, but he's also tuned into reality. He believes in himself. He's discovered who he is, and he knows where he's going. He doesn't expend all his energy on one area of his life; he gives attention to all of it. He knows that if his life gets out of balance, he'll find himself knee-deep in mud.

The winner is enthusiastic about life and living. He knows that most baseball games are won by only a couple of runs, and most horse races are won by a few steps. He knows that most football coaches attribute their wins or losses to whether or not their teams were "up" for the game—to their enthusiasm. The successful person knows that while enthusiasm isn't essential for getting a job done, it *is* essential for getting it done in the best possible way.

The success-minded person knows that he's unique. He's not a photocopy but an original. He doesn't compare himself to others. He doesn't compete with Jones down the street, only with himself. He wants to be better than he was five years ago, and better than he was six months ago.

He concentrates on running his own race rather than someone else's, because there's a far greater chance of winning his own. He knows that his body, soul, and spirit are the work of God, and that there is a piece of the Master within. He knows that he sculpts his own masterpiece.

The person geared toward winning loves himself. He has high self-esteem coupled with a knowledge of self-worth. He loves who he is, and he doesn't sit around daydreaming, wishing he were in someone else's shoes. He accepts himself for who he is, even after he knows himself for what he is. He knows he's a creature of the Creator, and that he is loved.

Loving others is a key to life, but you can't love others unless you love yourself. The Bible says, "Love your neighbor *as yourself*." You *can't* love others unless you love yourself.

This, Too, Will Change

A successful person judges himself strictly and has great discipline in his life. At the same time, however, he forgives himself for his shortcomings. He knows he's less than perfect and always will be. He doesn't condemn himself because he knows that self-condemnation is a great barrier to success. He doesn't live in guilt over past events, but rather picks himself up and moves on, even if he falls seven times. He deals with life's situations in the best possible way; then he moves on without looking back.

The winner cries over every failure—once! He rejoices over every victory—once! Then he moves on. He looks toward the future while giving today everything he's got. He looks ahead expectantly. He exercises faith, and thereby excludes all doubt. Where faith resides, doubt is automatically evicted! It's impossible for them to be co-tenants.

The successful person knows he must be able to roll with the punches of life and adapt to the changes that inflict themselves upon him. He knows that change is running rampant in our world, and failure to cope with this change can be a disaster. He knows he must learn to cope creatively. He knows he must continue to grow, because everything that is not growing is either dead or dying.

The successful person knows he must learn to be happy, but he knows that happiness doesn't come from circumstances. Let's face facts: Most things are incapable of making us happy. Happiness must come from within to be genuine. It is the joy that flows *from within*, where you know you're right with yourself and with God.

The successful person knows that all pleasure is only temporary, and that everything, including life itself, will draw to its own conclusion. Whether something is good or bad, we must come to grips with the fact that *this too will change.*

The Greatest Failure

The winner accepts what he cannot change. He knows that some things are out of his control. He's also free to fail. He knows that failure doesn't mean *he* is a failure. He recognizes that failure is merely an avenue for greater development and maturity. (We learn faster from our mistakes than from any success!)

According to the success-standards of most people, Jesus Christ was one of the greatest failures in all of history. He never owned a home or any of the other material aspects of life which we hold so dear. He had to walk almost every place he went because he didn't have a horse or donkey. And he died the death of a criminal. Even his closest friends denied him and deserted him.

Just the opposite was Napoleon Bonaparte. This great French general was one of the greatest successes the world has ever seen. He was wealthy. He was feared. He was admired. He was a conqueror with almost unequaled authority, and he held the power of life and death in his hands. Yet, it was Napoleon who said:

I know men, and I tell you that Jesus Christ was no mere man. Between him and every other person in the world there is no possible term of comparison. Alexander, Caesar, Charlemagne, and I have founded empires. But on what did we rest the creations of our genius? Upon force. Jesus Christ founded his empire upon love, and at this hour millions of men would die for him.

What is success to you? We all need to define success as we personally relate to it and what it means to us. Jesus' definition was far different from the one held by Napoleon. Similarly, my definition will be different from yours. We each must set our priorities and decide what is important for us in our own particular experience of life.

We each must decide what we believe about life and living. We each must choose the attitude with which we're going to respond to life. We must decide who and what we're going to serve. (We are indeed creatures of habit, but we have total freedom to choose what we'll be slaves to!) And even though we can't see the end of the parade, we need to plan our entire lives.

Consult the Author of Life

There is a doctrine in our American system of jurisprudence that says "Ignorance of the law is no defense." You are presumed to know the law, whether or not you actually do. Likewise, we must choose to be knowledgeable about life and not to react out of simple ignorance. Avoiding reality is at best foolishness; at worst, I truly believe that people can be destroyed by lack of knowledge. Don't turn your back on the truth about yourself and your world!

Create a list of priorities right now. At the very top of that list, write as your primary goal: "Come to grips with life." Then: "Decide what success and failure mean to me." This is the groundwork upon which you can build. Don't build on the shifting sand of some untested worldly philosophy—human philosophies today are a dime a dozen! Most of them have a piece of the truth, but all of them will get you knee-deep in mud if you're not careful!

To find out about life, simply consult the Author of Life. What better place to go to find out about a product than to consult the manufacturer of that product? Similarly, what better place to find out about life than to consult the Book of Life? The Bible is indeed the Manufacturer's Handbook!

I'd like to leave you with one thought that helped to

change my life and just might change yours, too. It comes from Charlie Jones's book, *Life Is Tremendous:* If the Bible is wrong, the believer has nothing to lose; but if the Bible is right, the unbeliever has everything to lose.

GINI GRAHAM SCOTT, Ph.D.

Working with the imagination has always been natural for Dr. Gini Graham Scott. She has been involved in imaginative and creative projects ever since she went into the business of selling worms and promoting them with comic book premiums at the age of six.

Her most recent project is a company called Creative Communications and Research, which provides numerous client services including writing, research, organizational design, program evaluation, proposal development, photography, film-making, graphics, and consulting. Dr. Scott also leads workshops on developing and using your imagination, doing research, and marketing yourself.

After earning her B.A. in 1963, Dr. Scott spent two and a half years as a project director in marketing research with an advertising agency. She then began her own business designing and manufacturing board games. Her imagination and marketing skills paid off in the form of more than two dozen games which she sold to major companies such as Pressman Toy, Hasbro Industries, Mag-Nif, and Skor-Mor. She also produced and distributed four other games herself.

In 1976 Dr. Scott was awarded a Ph.D. in sociology. She is now doing post-doctoral work in anthropology, teaching sociology at several San Francisco Bay Area colleges, and writing and researching for numerous clients.

Dr. Scott is the originator of a program called "Visions," which works with developing the imagination and creativity using a process of guided imagination techniques and group sharing. She has also written numerous articles on this topic. Her book on the recent cult phenomenon, *Cult and Countercult,* was recently published by Greenwood Press.

Dr. Scott has made numerous radio and television appearances and was featured on her own Bay Area radio program. She has led workshops and given presentations throughout the country to groups which include the International Platform Association, Toastmasters, the Lions Club, Women Entrepreneurs, the American Anthropology Association, the University of California, San Francisco State University, and West Georgia College.

You may contact Dr. Scott by writing to Creative Communications and Research, 1314 La Loma, Berkeley, CA 94708; or telephone (415) 845-1649.

PUT YOUR IMAGINATION TO WORK

AND GET WHATEVER YOU WANT

by

GINI GRAHAM SCOTT, Ph.D.

Your imagination can be an idea gold mine, and you can put it to work to get whatever you want. Your imagination can help you relax when you're jittery, wake you up when you're sluggish, and give you the insight to make that crucial decision. You can use your imagination to break habits, understand others, improve relationships, and plan ahead. In short, you can mobilize your imagination to decide what you want and direct your energy toward getting it.

I'm going to describe some mental techniques I've used successfully for the past 15 years in my own work as a writer, researcher, teacher, and consultant and have shared with others in workshops. What I term imagination is the power to see, hear, and feel internally. The underlying principle is that you can learn to direct this power to achieve your ends. It takes only 15 to 20 minutes a day to apply these techniques, and the more you work with them, the more proficient you'll become.

Our culture stresses the use of reason or logic. Much of the time rational thought works well. But there are times when it doesn't. At such times you can get better results by putting aside your logic and using imagination to get in touch with your inner wisdom.

After you've used these techniques for a while you can use them anywhere—even in a rush-hour crowd. But in the beginning, a quiet place is probably best. And if you use one place regularly, that's even better. You'll come to associate it with using your inner powers, and that will help you to mobilize them.

LEARNING TO RELAX

Relaxation is basic to each of these techniques. Prior to using any one of them you will spend a preparation period to relax. Here are two methods you can use to promote relaxation. Allow two or three minutes for each and begin by lying down or seating yourself in a comfortable chair. You may want to keep a notebook or tape recorder handy to keep track of the insights that may come to you.

1. Focus on Your Breathing

Close your eyes and pay attention to your breathing. Notice how your breath goes in and out, and concentrate only on this for about one minute. Then, with each inhalation, imagine your breath flowing to a different point in your body. Breathe down to your neck, to your hand, to your foot and be aware of your breath flowing in and out. Repeat to yourself several times: "I am relaxed; I am relaxed; I am relaxed."

2. Calm Your Body

Use this approach when your body feels tense. Close your eyes and pull every muscle in your body as tight as you can. Clench your feet, arms, legs, jaws, and stomach muscles. Then release all your muscles, letting them go limp. Repeat this step several times.

Then, starting from your feet and working your way up to your head, concentrate on warming and relaxing each body part. Say to yourself: "My toes are now warm and relaxed; my feet are now warm and relaxed; my legs are now warm and relaxed. ..." Conclude by telling yourself: "Now I am totally calm, totally relaxed." You may want to repeat this procedure several times.

INCREASING YOUR ENERGY

If you're feeling tired, lethargic, or unmotivated, here are two techniques to wake you up. You can use them to tap your inner energy reserves and to direct energy wherever you wish. Whether for writing a report, holding a meeting, teaching a class, or running a mile, these techniques will give you an energy boost.

1. Create Your Own Energy

Use this technique to increase your energy level. Stand with your feet slightly apart and make a tight fist with one hand. Quickly raise your fist above your head and lower it again. Do this several times, shouting out with as much enthusiasm as you can muster: "I am awake!" or "I am energy!" Feel the energy surge through you. (If it is not appropriate for you to do this physically, visualize the experience in your mind's eye.)

2. Direct Your Energy

Use this technique to prepare yourself to embark on some project. Sit with your spine straight, your feet firmly on the floor, and your eyes closed. Open your hands, palms up, to receive energy.

Now see the energy of the earth rise from the ground and surge into your body. Be aware that this energy is strong and solid. Feel it rise through your feet, your legs, your spine, and then expand out into your torso, arms, and head. See the strength of this energy becoming your strength.

As earth energy surges through you, energy from the air enters the top of your head. Be aware that this energy is light and expansive. Visualize it coursing down through your head into your spine and your arms, spiraling down through your torso. Imagine this energy making you light and buoyant.

The two energies meet at the base of your spine. See them combine and spiral up and down your spine together, radiating their energy through you.

Experience this spiraling energy for one or two minutes, until you feel filled with energy. Then visualize the energy surging outward into the project you want to accomplish. Begin the task at hand with that picture in your mind.

MAKING DECISIONS

Decisions are often difficult because there are so many factors to consider; sometimes all the alternatives seem equally attractive. This is the time to draw on your inner wisdom and let the decision flow from your intuition or gut feelings. Here are two techniques to help you make decisions.

1. Let Your Body Decide

If your decision involves a simple *yes/no* or *go/no-go* response, you can look to your own body for the answers. Do this exercise physically at first. Then, after you are accustomed to doing it, you can visualize it in your mind's eye.

Take some extra time to prepare when you are trying this exercise for the first time. Then begin, stand straight, and imagine your body as a pendulum. Sway backward and forward. This means *yes.* Now sway to the right and left. This means *no.* Sway in a circular motion. This means *maybe* or *ask again*—you're not sure or can't answer now.

Practice these motions and become familiar with the signals. Practice by asking yourself some *yes* or *no* question to which you know the answer. Your body should respond appropriately. Once it does so consistently, you are ready to use this technique to get answers.

Ask your questions very clearly. Don't try to move your body in any direction—let it move by itself and observe how it responds.

Normally, you should get a clear *yes* or *no.* If you don't, it is an indication that either you are not asking the question clearly, or you are not ready to decide. Another possibility is that you may be letting your consciousness get in the way. Either relax more to set aside your conscious mind, or reframe your question and ask it again when you have more information.

2. Take a Mental Journey to Get Your Answers

If your question involves more than a simple *yes* or *no* answer, it may be helpful to go on an inner journey to meet the part of you that has the answers.

Find a comfortable place to sit and relax your body. Then see yourself in a beautiful meadow with a large mountain in the distance. Begin walking to that mountain, and observe the countryside as you go. Travel slowly and try to experience everything you see.

A path winds up to the top of the mountain. Walk up the path. Look about as you climb, and be aware that you are leaving the meadow far behind and entering another world.

At the top of the mountain you notice a small hut. This is the home of a wise man who is said to know the answers to all things. As you approach the house, think of one or two questions you wish to have answered. Knock on the door.

When the wise man opens the door, you ask your first question. He thinks for some time, then answers. Listen carefully to what he says.

Now ask any other questions you may have. When the wise man has completed his reply, go back down the mountain to the meadow and open your eyes.

INCREASE YOUR SELF-CONFIDENCE AND SELF-ESTEEM

Your imagination can be a great confidence and esteem builder. If you're feeling low, anxious, or fearful; if you're worried that you can't do something; if you want to impress someone special—use your imagination to bolster your confidence. It can help you to successfully meet any upcoming challenges and feel good about yourself again. (In fact, a little imaginative esteem-building each day can work like preventive medicine to keep those doubts away and reaffirm your belief in your own marvelous being!)

Here are five approaches you can use: (1) Remind

yourself of your good qualities, talents, and accomplishments; (2) Affirm that you have certain qualities you want to develop; (3) See yourself successfully achieving some goal and being recognized for your efforts; (4) Rehearse an upcoming experience in your mind; and (5) Take control of the situation and setting.

1. Remember Your Successes

You'll need a sheet of paper and a pencil for this one. Close your eyes and for the next five minutes think about one of the following topics: "My Good Qualities," "What I'm Good At," or "My Accomplishments."

Each time an idea comes to mind, write it down. See how many qualities and accomplishments you can list.

Then review your list. As you read each item, close your eyes and experience how good it feels to have that quality. Realize that you have a lot going for you.

2. See Yourself With the Qualities You Want

You are, and you become, what you think. So imagine yourself with the qualities you want, and you'll develop them.

The secret is using affirmations. Select an affirmation that describes your objectives, word it so it is happening now, and meditate on it. Try it for just a few minutes a day for a week, and notice how you start to change! Some examples of affirmations:

- I am self-confident.
- I see the world as a wonderful, positive place.
- I know what I want and I can get it.
- I am charming and poised.

- I am exciting, energetic, and dynamic.
- I am strong and powerful.
- I am outgoing and attract people to me.

3. Visualize Your Success

Since success builds self-esteem, visualizing success will cause your self-esteem to grow.

To begin, decide what goal you want to achieve. Then relax, close your eyes, and vividly imagine yourself realizing that goal. If your goal is to perform well on the job, see yourself completing your tasks perfectly. Hear your supervisor praising you. Experience good feelings.

If your goal is to do well on a test, see yourself taking that exam and knowing all the answers. Imagine yourself writing them down quickly, and feel the confidence that comes with having knowledge.

If your goal is to establish a successful relationship with someone you want to do business with, see yourself contacting that person to work on a joint project. Visualize yourself sharing many ideas, and see your business partner responding positively to them. Experience the successful completion of the project. Whatever your goal, use your imagination to visualize what you want and see yourself achieving that goal.

4. Experience the Event in Advance

Suppose you have an important occasion coming up and want to excel. One way to become more confident, assertive, and dynamic in real life is to play out the role in your mind in advance.

Close your eyes and relax. Imagine yourself in the situation you're concerned about. Pay attention to the surroundings, the sounds, who's there, and what's going on. Say what you expect to say. Act as you will want to act. Rehearse your part in your mind and notice that you are entirely cool and confident, and that you express yourself flawlessly and effortlessly. Notice that everyone responds well to you.

Or as a variation on this technique, see yourself as an expert on some topic. Visualize yourself talking about your area of expertise on a radio talk show, in front of a class, or to a group of associates. Rehearse your role as an authority.

Repeat this visualization just before your big moment arrives. Then, as you perform in reality, keep in mind the feeling of confidence you have already experienced.

5. Take Control of the Situation

This technique will help you feel self-assured in unfamiliar surroundings and unusual circumstances.

Whenever you enter an area where you feel unsure of yourself (such as a room filled with strangers), visualize columns of energy flowing into your body from the earth. Then imagine lines of energy radiating out from you to the four corners and the ceiling of the room.

As you walk about or talk to people in the room, feel this energy move with you and radiate from you. Notice that this energy fills you with power and spreads your power throughout the room, so that you exude self-assurance and confidence.

BREAKING BAD HABITS

You can use your imagination to make undesirable habits fade away. The key is to make sure you really *want* to change. Then chase the habit away by developing a strong dislike for it or repeatedly visualizing yourself with the habit gone.

1. Do You Really Want to Break It?

Sometimes you may want to give up a habit because you think you should or because someone else wants you to. But at the same time, down deep you may really cling to that habit.

For example, suppose you think you want to give up smoking. It could be that most of your friends smoke. Perhaps you find that holding a cigarette relaxes you in a social situation. So, although you may say that you want to give up smoking, there are at least two factors that may prevent you from doing so. In order to stop smoking you'll have to decide that not smoking is more important to you than experiencing that relaxed feeling or doing what most of your friends do.

There may actually be times that you will be better off *with* a bad habit than without it. For instance, if you are truly awkward without a cigarette in social situations, perhaps it might be better for you to continue smoking—at least until you find an effective substitute. Whatever your circumstance, this technique will help you discover what you really want.

To begin, use the basic pendulum technique for making decisions. See yourself as a pendulum that swings forward and back for *yes*, right and left for *no*, and in a circle for *maybe* or *ask again*. Then ask these questions:

- Do I really *want* to give up this habit?
- Am I ready to give it up *now?*
- Is it in my *best interest* to give it up?

If you get all *yeses*, work on breaking that habit. If you get some *noes*, ask why. You may have some good reasons for holding onto your habit, and if so, honor them until the time comes when you are really *ready* to get rid of it.

2. Hate It

If you want to get rid of a habit, make yourself truly detest it. Close your eyes, relax, and meditate on the question: "Why is this habit bad for me?" Imagine all the bad things you can about this habit. Then imagine that they are happening to you.

(If your habit is smoking, you might see yourself in the throes of a coughing fit while you are delivering a speech.)

3. See It Gone

If you think you already hate your habit enough, you can skip over the previous technique and go directly to this one. However, these two techniques are like the carrot and the stick. Either can work by itself, but they are usually more effective when used together.

The basic approach is simple. See yourself clearly without your bad habit, and see yourself reaping all sorts of benefits. Be aware that without the habit, you feel joyous and free. You feel a sense of accomplishment for having gotten rid of your habit. Maybe your friends will notice the difference in your behavior and praise your achievement. Visualize all the prizes that will be yours.

GETTING TO KNOW OTHERS BETTER

Techniques for understanding other people are valuable not only in developing relationships, but in dealing with others in a business setting.

Outward appearances—including clothes, gestures, and word choices—give clues to what is inside the person. But you can also use your powers of imagination to tap your inner wisdom and tell you what that person is really thinking and feeling.

You can use your imagination to help you in three ways:

- To get a preview of a person before you meet him.

- To size up a person when you meet.

- To get further insights into the person you are dealing with.

1. Getting Advance Impressions

You can be better prepared for that all-important first meeting if you have a general idea of what to expect from the person. The key is getting an overall intuitive impression of the person's personality type, since each type reacts favorably to different characteristics and actions.

There are four basic personality types.

- *The Intuitive.* This type is assertive, aggressive, and direct—the ideal leader. The Intuitive likes other people to support his ideas and be direct and to the point.

- *The Visionary.* The Visionary is cool, calm, detached, and independent. He likes to analyze, to understand how things fit together. He likes others to be clear, well-organized, and analytical, and to provide a full picture.

- *The Feeler.* This person is very sensitive, emotional, and dependent on others. He likes details and is concerned that things run smoothly. He likes people who provide details, and who are warm, feeling, and responsive.

- *The Knower.* This type is very perceptive, and often feels that he knows it all. The Knower is frequently critical, judgmental, and opinionated. But since he has a good sense of how things will turn out, he tends to be a good planner and organizer. The Knower is especially responsive to people who are organized, self-assured, confident, and accepting of his ideas.

Once you have gained insight into the type of person you are going to meet, you can act in a manner calculated to produce a favorable response.

To find out what type of person you will be dealing with, relax. Close your eyes and see the image or the name of the person you are going to meet. Watch the image or name expand and contract until it becomes a pulsating ball of energy, swirling around in a circle.

As you watch, a word appears to describe that person's personality type—Intuitive, Visionary, Feeler, or Knower. (If more than one word appears, the person is a combination of both types.)

Keeping the word and its associated traits in mind, visualize yourself meeting that person and using the appropriate approach. Later, this mental warm-up will help you make a good impression.

2. Sizing Up the People You Meet

The key to knowing another person well is to pay attention to the images, words, or sensations you feel when you first meet. These are clues to his deepest character.

When you first shake hands with someone, notice the first image, word, or feeling that comes to your mind.

Then, while you talk, think about what that image means to you. If the picture of a tiger comes into your mind, you might be reminded of the qualities of aggression, tenacity, or slyness. These associations will suggest things that you should take into account when relating to that person.

3. Getting Deeper Insights

Insight into how others will act or react in various situations can help you deal with them effectively. This identification technique will deepen your insights and help you to sense other people's expectations and attitudes.

Close your eyes and relax. Then visualize the person as if he were standing or seated directly in front of you. Look at his face carefully for about a minute. Notice his eyes, lips, bone structure, chin. Then, in your imagination, stretch out your arms, lift his head from his body, and place it on your own shoulders.

Imagine that you have become this person. Look at the world through his eyes. Take note of what you see, hear, and feel. Then ask yourself questions to find out how *he* would act, think, or feel in various situations.

You might ask questions like: "What do I want in an employee?" or "What is most important to me?"

Other questions might be: "What do I look for in someone I want to promote?" "How do I like people to dress?" "What kind of conversations do I most enjoy?" "What kind of behaviors or accomplishments impress me the most?"

Don't try to answer consciously. Let the answers come without effort.

After you finish your questions, return the head to the other person's body and open your eyes.

IMPROVING YOUR RELATIONSHIPS WITH OTHERS

You can use your imagination to make your relationships

with others proceed more smoothly. The next two techniques can help you to identify problems and their solutions. They can create the positive attitude that will enable you to relate better to the people you have problems with.

1. Resolving Problems

When something's wrong, you can create your own personal counselor in your imagination, then ask yourself for advice.

Start by getting comfortable. Relax and close your eyes. Then visualize yourself going along a path in the woods to your dream house. Enter the house, look around, and explore.

Toward the back of the house a door leads downstairs to your workshop. Go down the stairs and enter the room. Notice that there is a long desk. On it is a computer-like console with numerous buttons to press, and above this is a large television screen.

Sit down at the console and press a button to summon your counselor. When he appears on the screen, describe your problem. If the answer is simple, your counselor will reply briefly. If the answer is complex, he will ask you to push a button and watch the screen. Then you will see an enactment of the solution.

To ask additional questions, simply press a button to summon back your counselor. Then, when you are finished, push the *off* button. Leave the workshop, go upstairs, and out through the door. As you walk down the path, return to normal consciousness.

2. Relating More Positively

Sometimes you have to work with or spend time with

someone you don't like. You can use your imagination to smooth things over—or even to turn your feelings around.

The key is to take some time to think positively about that person. At first, this may be hard to do. Practice by meditating on his good qualities, trying to put aside any feelings about his bad qualities. Finally, visualize yourself sending positive feelings to him.

When you see that person again, you'll respond to him more positively, and he will also respond better to you.

PLANNING AHEAD

The only certainty today is change. If you can get some insight into how change will affect you, you will be better prepared for it. Or better yet, you can plan ahead for the changes you *want* to occur. You can set goals.

Looking Into the Future

This technique involves visualizing yourself at various stages in your life to see where you are going.

Close your eyes, relax, and imagine yourself in a train station. The train pulls into the station and you get aboard. You realize that this is no ordinary train; its tracks run into the future.

You are taking this train to some future destination. Notice that the countryside you pass is very ordinary, but when you pull into the first station, the sign says "One Month in the Future." Below the sign is a large screen. Observe what appears on the screen: Where are you now? What are you doing? Are you making any changes in your life?

Then the train pulls away and travels through the

countryside to the next station. This time the sign says "Three Months in the Future." Ask the same questions, and again notice what appears on the screen.

The train moves on once more. This time imagine that the sign says whatever you want: "Six Months in the Future," "One Year in the Future," "Five Years," whatever.

Travel on the train until you have gone as far ahead in time as you like. Then, take the train back to the present and open your eyes.

Use the insights from your train ride to help you plan where you are going.

And Now You're on Your Own

The preceding exercises are just some of the many imagination techniques you can use to get what you want. You can modify the imagery or create your own exercises to suit your own goals and needs. The only requirement is that you let go of your rational, logical mind, so that you can get in touch with your intuition.

You must learn to relax, focus your attention inward, be receptive and positive, and allow your imagination to respond freely, without trying to direct or control its responses. You use the insights you receive to help you direct and control in real life.

Notice the changes that occur when you work with these techniques. You'll find that many positive things happen. And when you put out positive energy, that's what you'll get back. Try it and see!

ARTHUR C. MOKAROW, Ph.D.

Art Mokarow is unique. He was an early standout success in the business and management field. Then his desire to motivate and inspire people led him to counseling, teaching, and public speaking. He brings to the platform decades of experience spiced with an unusual amount of compassion and understanding.

But he's not just a good lecturer and he's not just a skilled counselor. With his repertoire of fascinating topics, he makes subjects of universal interest come alive for one and all. He doesn't tell fairy tales. He deals with reality; but he makes it fun. Even though his audiences may see their problems and challenges in a new and brighter light, he makes them feel stronger and more capable of meeting their problems.

Art Mokarow heads his own human development consulting firm, AM Consultants. He is a graduate in education from both DePaul University and Ambassador College. He completed his doctorate in counseling at Pacific States University in Los Angeles and did graduate work at the University of Southern California.

He was listed in *Who's Who in American Colleges and Universities.* He belongs to the American Association of University Professors and International Platform Speakers Association and is on the board of the Pasadena Council on Alcoholism.

He has spent 10 successful years in sales and business management. He also has a composite of 20 years in the field of counseling and is certified by the Carbon County Mental Health Center as an intern in Marriage and Family Counseling. His specialties are speaking and training and he has lectured and consulted for state associations, prisons, commercial corporations, professional groups, the handicapped, and charitable organizations nationally and internationally.

You can contact Art Mokarow by writing to him at P.O. Box 2811, Pasadena, CA 91105; or telephone (213) 799-1828. He is represented by William Behrer, (212) 244-1555.

THE LAWS
OF ACHIEVEMENT

by ARTHUR C.
MOKAROW, Ph.D.

The old television show *The Millionaire* appealed to the universal appetite for getting something for nothing.

The central figure in the show was the executive secretary and confidant of a philanthropic multibillionaire who each week gave away one million dollars to a selected needy individual. There was a stipulation that recipients tell no one how they received the money. They could spend the money in any way they chose, so long as they didn't reveal the circumstances of their good fortune. Each recipient believed that his financial windfall would enable him to achieve all his personal goals.

Each week the series pictured how joy turned into confusion and anxiety as recipients tried to spend their fortune and keep the secret. In the end, the million dollars which seemed to be the magic solution to all problems became an even greater problem. What looked like a sure road to success was a path to disappointment.

This TV program proved that achievement can't be bought. Achievement occurs only when we follow the *laws* of achievement. To attain success we need to know and implement those rules.

A doctor once developed a product that was guaranteed to make his personal fortune and insure his material happiness. Having noticed that laboratory tests showed common tap water to contain harmful chemicals, he invented a filtering device.

Anticipating exceptional need for his invention, he invested heavily in the marketing and manufacturing of the product. He expected it to be an overnight success. But his plan failed and he was financially ruined. After much struggling to keep his head above water, he finally admitted defeat and declared bankruptcy.

What went wrong? He had thought there was no way he could miss. Why didn't this man achieve his dream?

At times all of us see our high hopes dashed to the ground. We plan to the best of our ability. We set a realistic goal, obtain adequate financing, and enlist competent, motivated support—and we still fail. Why does this happen?

In my counseling experience I have heard many reasons for failure. They range from "We had a cash-flow problem," to "The time wasn't right." The reasons that people give to explain their failures are always valid to some degree. But how is it that *other people* with the same obstacles overcome them and achieve their goals? How do some people turn obstacles into stepping stones to success?

The answer is that the successful people are doing something the failures are not. *They are following different rules.*

The doctor, like the new millionaires on the TV show, lacked knowledge of the hidden laws of achievement. These inflexible rules are as real and as meaningful as the very laws of nature.

RULE 1:
INHERENT IN EVERY SOLUTION ARE ITS FUTURE PROBLEMS

Successful people adhere to this rule from the very beginning; they make provision for it in the initial planning of action. Inexperienced people often ignore this rule, thereby limiting their chances of success.

A typical example of this occurs when a manufactured product is offered on a market that clamors for more. There may not be adequate supplies to keep up with the demand. Then shortage of supplies becomes an unexpected obstacle. Because the problem wasn't anticipated, it cannot be dealt with.

We need to understand the dynamics of this rule if we are to appreciate its use. Human beings function by systems, clearly delineated steps for moving from point to point. Whenever we lack a method for dealing with an obstacle, it's an indication that our present system for going from point A to point B—of getting things done— just doesn't work.

Garbage In, Garbage Out

Systems basically encompass three categories: input, storage, and output. If the input is erroneous, then what is stored and finally produced will be faulty. The jargon for this in the computer field is "Garbage in, garbage out."

This concept is the basis of our modern computer systems. The programmer is a vital link assuring that a system performs properly. It is the programmer's responsibility to feed accurate data and methodology into the computer's memory bank.

We are our own computer programmers. Whenever we function according to a plan and fail, we can identify our problem as one of input: our data and methods must be in error.

When we succeed in developing a system that works, we will experience success so long as conditions remain *exactly the same*. But change is the one real constant in the human experience. Continually changing conditions alter the validity of our data. Hence, Rule 1: *We are always confronted with new problems to solve.*

Considering Rule 1 means always being prepared for the unexpected. To avoid systems breakdowns we need to pre-program our solutions to handle future contingencies. Once we analyze our solutions as problem-producers and make the proper alterations in our system, we can then resume moving toward our goal.

Internal and External Conditions

There are two major areas of changing conditions, internal (generated by our cognition and thinking) and external (outside of our control). Changing your mind is an example of an internal change. A sudden storm is an example of an external change. Either could affect your plan of action.

The entire universe is affected by change. Whenever we alter a system to solve a problem, that change affects the whole. Whenever we change our plans in order to reach our goals, we cause others to adapt and change accordingly. Whatever happens to one affects all.

One example of this is the gasoline shortage. Let's say you and your family for years have vacationed in the mountains of Wyoming. The trip is one that the entire family looks forward to as part of the family's system of entertainment.

As the fuel shortage creates higher prices, the journey becomes too costly. A change in fuel availability—an external condition—has affected you and your whole family.

Indeed, the fuel shortage affects the entire nation. How could Rule 1 have been applied to avoid negative consequences?

If the auto manufacturers had considered that their solution of mass-producing assembly line vehicles for our nation would ultimately produce fuel problems, they might have prepared for the inevitable. Had they made research and development a priority, it is probable that alternative fuels would now be in use and modified vehicles would achieve better mileage.

Remember that every solution to a problem *has the capacity to create a new problem*. And a problem prepared for is 50 percent easier to handle than an unexpected one. You can increase your chances for success by diagnosing the problem, surveying the potential *future difficulties*, and preparing for them.

RULE 2:
ALL LOGIC IS NOT TRUTH

How often do we dash off into the future, certain we are right, because something seems *logical*? And how many times do we meet with failure? One of the most damaging obstacles to success is acting on the impression that something makes sense, when additional information could reveal its fallacies.

Rational thought is highly prized in our culture. It makes us susceptible to believing that *whatever appears to make sense must be true*.

109

Single people may see getting married as the logical solution to loneliness. When they find a mate and marry, they believe their loneliness is over. Only then do they discover, to their chagrin, that being *alone* and being *lonely* are two different things.

It "makes sense" to think, "If I feel lonely it's because I'm alone. If I'm not alone, then I won't be lonely." This is similar to saying that one plus one makes two. It's only logical. (Yet mathematicians have told me that one plus one does *not always* make *exactly* two!)

What is the problem with this type of reasoning? Why isn't logic always true? Let's analyze this example.

In this situation, as is commonly the case, all the facts were not known. Perhaps one of the partners was unable to relate adequately to another person; perhaps the other was unwilling to deal with conflict. Those factors, which were not considered in advance, played a substantial part in undermining the effectiveness of the marriage.

Most scientific findings are spoken of as *theoretical* rather than *absolute.* This is an admission that based on the known facts and known conditions a certain result *should* follow—but that it could possibly be changed by new or yet unknown facts.

As we move in the direction we think to be logical and true, *it's important to test our logic,* just as the scientist experiments to substantiate his theories.

RULE 3:
ALWAYS HAVE AN ALTERNATIVE

The Russian campaigns of Napoleon and Hitler clearly point out the need for following this rule. Both men attacked without adequate reserves of manpower and supplies. They were so certain of victory that they failed to consider the great stress that would be placed on their armies and supply lines by the severe Russian winters. The prolonged campaigns left them open to defeat by hunger and cold.

Putting all your eggs in one basket is never wise. How many individuals enter business with little financial support, run into difficulties, and then fold for lack of money? When you start a venture without alternatives, you decrease your chances for success before you even start.

A sound plan of action would be to begin with both adequate capital and a back-up system—a lending institution and friends, besides—to provide emergency reserves. Then, in the event that unexpected cash-flow problems were to develop, you would have some viable alternatives.

The need for alternatives would not be so imperative if it were possible to make the temporary be permanent, as so many of us try to do. We often act as if today will last forever.

The middle-aged woman who experiences the "empty nest" syndrome is a typical example of this problem. It is a common experience for a mother to invest so much of her personal identity in her children that she feels abandoned when they leave home.

It's *inevitable* that children will grow up and pursue their adult lives, and therefore it's essential for young mothers to plan their lives with the awareness that their children's dependency needs are temporary, not permanent. Women with children must begin early to seek out and build other identity support systems for themselves.

Each time we try to give perpetuity to the temporary we have assured ourselves of a future crisis.

RULE 4:
NEEDS ARE GREATER THAN WANTS

Unless we clearly understand our personal goals we will have great difficulty in distinguishing between needs and wants. As opposed to desires, wishes, motivations, drives, and wants, *needs* are directly related to meaningful goals.

You might say that you would like to be rich. You have a *want* for wealth, but if your goal does not involve doing what is necessary to achieve wealth, then your want is not a need, and your chances of becoming rich are small.

Whether consciously or not, each of us selects his own needs. When our personal goals are not clearly defined, then our needs aren't clear, and our chances for failure are great.

As a sales manager for an insurance company, I used to recruit, select, train, and supervise insurance agents. In each case every new agent would say he wanted— *wanted*—to be a successful insurance agent. Even though they all *wanted,* some just didn't make it. Why not?

Motivation to do what needs to be done is directly linked to the intensity of the desire. Only when we want something badly enough do we see it as a need. Only then will we be willing to do what is necessary to achieve it.

When one speaks of dieting to lose weight he is really saying "What do I want most, to eat or to lose weight?" Only if the desire to lose weight is strong enough to cut down the food intake do we recognize that desire as not merely a want but a need.

To increase your achievement rate *make sure your goals are needs.*

RULE 5:
STAY OUT OF THE HOLE

When I was twelve, one of my most memorable experiences was swimming a rapid river. So long as I angled my swim diagonally across from one side to the other I avoided being caught by the current and washed downstream.

Then one day I broke my angle of direction and was immediately sucked under by the current. I felt myself plunging down a whirlpool to the river bed.

When I came to, I found myself being torn in different directions by the current. The bottoms of my tennis shoes were cut to ribbons on the rock bottom. After I finally broke to the surface of the water, nearly exhausted, I still had to swim to the other river bank. Fortunately, my youth provided sufficient energy reserves to carry me to safety.

One of the pitfalls in our path to achievement is allowing our desire to succeed to overpower our energy reserves. Sometimes we want so strongly to achieve our goals that we do the very opposite of what we should do. We concentrate so desperately on the final result that we lose sight of what we need to do to get there.

Taking examinations is a good example of this. Some people fail tests because they want so much to pass. They become nervous and anxious, and they lose the capacity to think effectively. This, in turn, makes them more anxious. They keep digging themselves deeper into the hole, and there they are stuck—for it takes more energy than they have to climb out again.

A better course of action in this case would be to temporarily change your goal from passing the test to relaxing. Then, when your anxiety level is lowered and you feel a surge of energy, having avoided the hole you would be free to again pursue the goal of passing the test.

Do It in Steps

When we are unaware that a job is too big for us we often begin and subsequently find it overwhelming. We need to recognize then that we're in a hole and it's going to take a lot of energy to get out. We need to re-evaluate our goals and analyze whether we will have enough energy to finish. If not, then a modification of our goal is in order.

Breaking down goals into sub-goals which are easily achieved is one method of dealing with this problem. We then can work away at our goal little by little until we finally achieve it. Doing it in small steps conserves energy and greatly increases the likelihood of success.

Avoid the Hole

If you can stay out of the hole entirely, you can apply all your energy to achieving your goal. How is it possible to do this?

Keep your goals clearly defined and crystal clear. Use measurable standards as guideposts to signal the pitfalls and show when you are on course. If you find yourself going the wrong way, immediately make the proper adjustments to keep on course.

A daily caloric intake limit serves as a prudent system to keep a dieter out of the hole. He knows that if he exceeds his 1200-calorie allowance one day, he has to make adjustments the next day in order to keep out of trouble. Without that measurable standard, weight loss would be virtually unattainable.

Avoid pitfalls by setting up systems which let you know where you stand *every step of the way* toward achievement.

RULE 6: FAIR IS FAIR

Probably of all these rules, this is the least used. What does this rule mean?

Nearly all that we do involves people. The very fact that our personal goals affect other people gives us a measure of responsibility. And whether other people help us or hinder us in attaining our goals depends to a large extent on whether *we affect them* positively, negatively, or neutrally.

In order for people to identify with us, we must deal with them fairly.

What Is Fair?

If we behave toward others according to what *we* think is fair, we are making unwarranted assumptions. What people expect from interpersonal relationships differs greatly from person to person.

Two young people choose to get married. Each loves the other. Each expects the other to be faithful, caring, and respectful. They look forward to a life of wedded bliss.

Six months later the young bride is disappointed because her husband doesn't pick his clothes up, come home on time for dinner, or fix the toaster.

The new husband in turn feels picked on, misunderstood, and unloved. He is tired of supporting the household. Both people feel cheated.

In this case, each person came into the marriage with a different set of expectations. The wife and the husband each believe that they are fulfilling their part of the marriage bargain. Both think they are not receiving what they should from the other party. Neither feels fairly treated.

If you want to increase your chances of success, you

must know exactly what other people expect from you. If you find yourself accumulating antagonists who hinder your achievement rate, find out what they expect from you. Fill their needs if possible. Then they will become partners in achieving your goals.

How to Be Fair

If one of the greatest errors we can make in dealing with others is assuming what will be considered fair, how can we avoid this error?

A good start is to improve our communication system. Do we really listen to others? Do we sense their personal needs? Do we know what their goals are? Have we heard *from them* what they expect of us?

Take time to listen. Explore the relationship and tell the other person what you perceive. Put out what you expect from him and ask what you can do to insure that your dealings with each other are fair.

The more we spell out what we mean by *fair*, the better our opportunity for success. For example, when you decide to buy an automobile, specify to the car dealer what you expect for the price the dealer is asking. Just because the car is stylish, sleek, racy and reasonably priced doesn't mean that the dealer will give you what you consider to be a fair deal. Let the dealer know that you expect to find all items working properly when the car is delivered and that any faulty items must be repaired without cost to you.

Be clear and definitive in your human relationships. *Fair for fair* eliminates the human obstacles to achievement.

•

As he helped me with this article, my son Kevin said,

"There is more to achievement than I could possibly have imagined!"

These six laws of achievement are only the beginning. Of course there are many more known laws, and there probably are others yet to be discovered. The impact, however, of using just these six can alter your success pattern toward new heights of achievement. Become aware of these hidden laws and respect them and you will experience the reality of true achievement!

HARRY E. GUNN, Ph.D.

Illinois psychologist Harry E. Gunn has been helping people deal with their fears since establishing his practice in 1966. He has counseled families in distress, consulted with educators in the management of emotionally disturbed children, facilitated sensitivity programs for industry, and led seminars for psychology interns on projective testing.

Dr. Gunn was educated at Beloit College, Purdue University, and Loyola University of Chicago, from which he was granted a Ph.D. in 1961. His areas of research include the analysis of thought processes, the measurement of problem-solving ability, and the possible relationships between height and personality traits among college freshmen. A report on his research on

Bender-Gestalt performance by culturally disadvantaged first graders appeared in *Perceptual and Motor Skills* in 1971.

Dr. Gunn has worked at identifying gifted children in ghetto areas, consulted for a school for the mentally handicapped, and evaluated managerial personnel. He was a consultant to the Office of Economic Opportunity's War on Poverty program in Pembroke and Kankakee, Illinois.

Dr. Gunn is affiliated with the American Psychological Association, the Illinois Psychological Association, the Florida Psychological Association, and the National Register of Health Service Providers in Psychology.

He lives with his wife Violet and their sons Buddy and Billy. He is the author of *Manipulation by Guilt* and co-author with Violet of *The Test Yourself Book*.

You may reach Harry E. Gunn by writing to 119 East Ogden Avenue, Suite 13B, Hinsdale, IL 60521; telephone (312) 654-3914.

TWO CAUSES
OF FAILURE:
FEAR OF SUCCESS AND
GUILT OVER SUCCESS

by HARRY E. GUNN, Ph.D.

"The man who felt guilty about success." This was how I used to think of a patient I saw many years ago. Charles Dean (as I'll call him) had requested my help because he always seemed to make a mess of his life. He said he had a rather good marriage and felt close to his children. That sounded healthy, and I wondered then what the problem might be.

Mr. Dean told me he'd always had a strong desire to do well in business. He wanted to work his way to the top. His life had been geared to advancement, and his wife had worked to help him.

Unfortunately, something always seemed to go wrong at the very moment that Dean had a good chance for promotion. It took five visits before I could put my finger on the source of his "bad luck." What was happening was that he was unconsciously *sabotaging* his own chances for success!

"Why can't I find success?" Most of us answer that question by reviewing our bad breaks, our lack of opportunity, and the failure of others to provide the help we need.

My clinical practice suggests that the actual cause of failure generally lies *within the person*. The old axiom that each of us is our own worst enemy is true. Like Mr. Dean, we sabotage ourselves. We throw away the success we want so very much. (It sounds crazy, doesn't it?)

The Price of Success

Let's take a look at the causes of such irrational behavior. First, consider: What is the price of success? When you experience success you will receive a mixed reaction from others. Some people may admire you but at the same time offer a thinly-veiled challenge: "Can you do it again?" People build idols but they love to see them fall. To this end, they may gradually undermine your confidence in very subtle ways.

Other people will be frankly jealous. They'll wonder how in the world you ever did it. They'll express the opinion that your success was no more than luck, or they may simply refuse to recognize your achievement. More than a few will imply that you don't deserve what you earned. These responses may begin to make you feel guilty about your success.

Guilt reactions can spring from another quarter, too. They can be prompted by your apparent admirers. They do recognize your success—and they talk about it constantly. And soon you begin to hear another message in their praise: They are saying, "*I* work hard, too! *I* deserve success, too!" You suddenly feel deflated and wonder if your success somehow took away the opportunity for others to be successful.

Finally, some people will feel angry about your achievements. ("How *dare* you make it when I can't?") They may attack you directly and behind your back. And if you defend yourself, you may be labeled "arrogant," "egotistical," or "touchy."

If this all seems a little paranoid, look at the evidence around you. Why were the New York Yankees so hated awhile back? Why are winning teams generally called "cold and methodical"? Why do people so often make critical comments about movie stars? ("She's really aged, hasn't she?" "He's much shorter than he seems on the screen.") When success produces so much negative reinforcement, no wonder we may unconsciously shy away from it!

The search for success, or its immediate prospect, also produces personal conflicts. But we do see their ramifications. It becomes difficult to get started. Every pencil must be razor sharp. We worry when things go too well. We experience creative block. It's so easy to become discouraged and quit.

The Two Big Fears

Why do we encounter all these difficulties? Let's examine some of the reasons. When we set out to meet a challenge, regardless of what it is, it's likely that our initial enthusiasm will be haunted by some degree of doubt. As the level of doubt rises, so does the degree of insecurity. We begin to feel less certain of succeeding. We doubt that we have the necessary talent for the job.

When our self-esteem is under attack, we all feel the need to defend our egos. One very simple defense is to say to ourselves that we *could* have been successful *if we had really tried.* By not putting out our full effort, we avoid the ego-crushing defeat we might have suffered had we given our all. Thus, when we postpone tackling a difficult objective we may be operating out of *fear of failure.*

Fear of success is another deterrent to achievement, and in many ways it is even more threatening than fear of failure. The more you have, the more there is to lose.

Many people have told psychologists about the vague uneasiness they experience when things go too well. They worry about when the ax will fall. And all of us fear the unknown. All of these factors may influence us to undermine our achievement.

Sometimes people go to great lengths to deny that they are fearful, and their bravado causes carelessness and insures ultimate failure. When failure finally does occur, they state that they knew it was coming all along. Now at least they have nothing to fear—or so they tell themselves.

Success can also add pressure, if we allow it to do so. After a noteworthy accomplishment the successful person feels elated. But his victory is likely to be short-lived in the eyes of others. Their judgments and criticisms are a dash of cold water. As he thinks about his success, a winner may begin to doubt his ability to repeat his fine performance. He may also recognize that he will have to accomplish more and more in order to impress the others. The taste of victory is pleasant, but with it comes the need to keep proving oneself. Little wonder that people are afraid of the burdens of success.

Any number of people may be described as overly dependent. They like to rely on others and generally shy away from decision-making and responsibility. This type of person is not likely to meet with success, but if he were to, think of the problems he would face! Making your own decisions can be very painful.

It's important to realize that there is a little of this kind of personality in all of us. It may seem needlessly difficult to succeed and stand alone, when we can more comfortably fail and lean.

Oh, the Guilt!

One of the most insidious causes of failure is guilt. We are all familiar with guilt over failure—but *guilt over success?*

If that seems unlikely, look at what happens on athletic fields. A successful team may be described as having "taken all the money away" from the other teams. A successful athlete is sometimes asked whether he might not have let someone else have a share of the limelight.

In the business world one sees the same pattern. The person who finds a shortcut is encouraged to feel guilty because someone else has to work longer hours for the same reward. Or he is told how much he owes to others. Success often causes us to feel guilty because we have more than other people have!

"What right do I have to expect an easy life?" we may ask. "Why do I deserve this, instead of *him?*" We may even come to the conclusion that our success should be taken away to make us equal to others!

If we believe that it isn't fair to have success when others experience failure, we will develop a great aversion to success. There may be unbearable guilt in realizing that we have apparently achieved more in life than our parents did.

One form of behavior which may result from such guilt reactions is a blocking of the creative processes. The person suddenly finds that he can no longer think creatively or he may take unnecessary chances and thereby experience ultimate failure. Then he is quick to give up and tell himself that he, too, can't win.

Overcoming the Obstacles

All of these psychological factors move a person away from success. We are led to ask whether this is inevitable or necessary. Do we have to be negatively influenced by psychological factors? Or is it possible to overcome the heavy psychological burden of guilt and anxiety? I believe that it is possible, that there are positive steps we can take to avoid these traps.

1. *Try to understand your motivation.* Understanding our unconscious motivation allows a more rational approach to life. What the human mind can see, the human mind can generally deal with. If you are not reaching your goals, you might find it worthwhile to put aside your natural defensiveness and talk to a friend or your spouse. They may be able to give you some insights into your own behavior. In some cases professional help may be in order.

2. *Review your goals.* Make certain that your priorities are your own—not someone else's. And be sure that you are willing to make the sacrifices that will be required to meet those goals. When you fail to accomplish what you set out to do, try to find out why. Try to understand what changes need to be made to insure success next time round. And then go on to win. Don't dwell on the failure.

3. *Notice how successful people operate.* You want to pattern yourself after winners, not losers. Whenever possible, select as models people who are successful in your own field. Learn how to draw from them the lessons you want to know. Learn to be a good listener and a good

talker. Rather than trying to prove your merits to others, ask key questions to elicit advice and information.

4. *Learn about yourself.* Find out what your talents are and where they can best be marketed. Don't try to do something you are unsuited for. Work toward your strengths. Tie your assets in with your goals. Don't create undue pressure for yourself by over-emphasizing failure; realize that no one wins all of the time. No one achievement or lack thereof should be the end of the world.

5. *Set short-term goals.* The right short-term goals will lead to your long-range goals. Goals that are too far distant may promote discouragement and procrastination. Shorter-term goals allow one to work at a steadier pace and provide for more immediate gratification.

6. *Try to avoid dependence on others.* Being independent allows you to set your own standards and be responsible for your own success or failure. It allows you more direct control of your destiny.

7. *Affirm the value of success.* Consider that our society needs successful people in order to survive and move ahead. Anyone who succeeds benefits other people as well. Regardless of what the "spoilers" may say, a society *follows leaders,* not failures. And a society needs leaders. Failures hurt everyone, particularly themselves.

Leaders set their own goals and make their own choices. Do you not choose to be moved by rational motives rather than propelled to defeat by self-destructive, irrational motivation?

The Man Who Felt Guilt Over Success

Here is how two individuals fought the battle and won. Charles Dean, the businessman with the advancement problem, ruined another good opportunity. He picked a fight with his wife in front of his boss, thus making a very bad impression. (How could he possibly handle other employees if he lost his temper so easily with his wife?)

As I talked to Dean he was positive that a big advancement had been "in the bag," prior to his verbal explosion. He admitted that he had started the fight. He said that at the time he had felt tense and nervous, but he wasn't sure why.

"Maybe things were going too well," he said jokingly.

"How so?" I asked.

"Well, my father always said that life is too easy for some people and those people never appreciate anything," he replied.

I asked Dean whether he felt that his life had been too easy, and suddenly I was hearing about all the sacrifices his father had made for him. He rambled on and on about the tough life his father had experienced, and how "Dad always wanted better for me." Dad had not taken vacations; he had worked all the time.

Gradually a pattern emerged. Dean felt the need to constantly express his gratitude to his father. In a sense, the more successful he was, *the more he would owe his dad!*

I asked him how he felt about his accomplishments. Did he remember how his father had reacted to his childhood achievements?

Dean recalled that he was a fine high-school athlete. He remembered when, as a sophomore, he had defeated a senior to win his first high-school swimming race. No one had expected him to win. His dad didn't attend the swim meet; he was working. And he didn't show much enthusiasm about it when he found out.

His father told him that as a boy he hadn't had much time for sports. "Sports may be fun," he said, "but they don't pay the bills."

It appeared that Dean's father paid recognition only to the accomplishments that fell in line with what *he* wanted. Otherwise the activity was deemed not worthwhile—and it surely didn't help pay father back for all that he had "done for his family"!

Later on in the therapy I tried to find out how Dean had expressed his anger. I've seen many youngsters who use underachievement to rebel against parental authority. It appeared, however, that such had generally not been the case with Mr. Dean. For the most part, father and son had a good relationship. Consequently Dean did not rebel against his father, but held his anger in.

Dean had heard one lecture over and over from his father. That was that one had to make sacrifices in order to get ahead. Success meant taking on even more responsibility and having to work increasingly harder, so as to avoid letting anyone down.

One day Dean revealed that he often felt angry when he moved up in his company. He was puzzled by this.

"Do you also feel guilt?" I asked.

Yes, he replied, he did feel guilt, but he wasn't sure why. It took this client a few more sessions to work out the whole pattern. He felt that he had advanced far beyond his hard-working father's accomplishments. Advancement brought him pleasures that his father had never experienced in his life of self-sacrifice, and this made him guilty. The guilt, in turn, by its injustice, made him angry. And it was this anger that showed itself in the form of quarrels and acrimonious remarks to his business superiors.

While Dean was consciously disappointed by failure to obtain his promotion, the unconscious side of his personality experienced secondary reward. If he failed to advance, then he needn't feel so indebted to his father.

This client was bright and well motivated and was

able to make quick personality changes as a result of his therapy. He is now a much freer person who enjoys life. He says that work comes easier to him now, as advancements certainly do.

The Woman Who Couldn't Decide

A second favorite of mine was a young woman whom I thought of as "The Woman Who Couldn't Decide." I'll call her Jan Davis. She was young, attractive, intelligent, talented, competitive, but also very confused. She decided on therapy as a means of straightening things out.

Davis had always felt that she knew what she wanted, but the key people in her life always wanted something else. She was continually torn between her need to be herself and her desire to make others happy.

The conflict that brought her into therapy centered on two very different behaviors. She was beginning to work her way up in an advertising agency and was the competent businesswoman that she appeared to be. At times, however, she acted like a silly, naive girl. This was very annoying to both her husband and her employer.

Davis was not at first sure what she was doing to alienate others. She had been accused of "acting a part," but the two roles were not apparent to her. I was not sure what was going on either, because I hadn't received a clear behavioral description from anyone who interacted with her.

However in one session in which I was trying to explain something to my client, the undesirable behavior showed itself. She had been arguing with me, and I had begun to realize that I was wrong. I started to tell her that, when she suddenly began to deny the validity of her own arguments. She acted childish, dependent, giggly, and illogical, and began to apologize for being correct!

I sat back and quietly watched her method of inter-acting with me. I noticed that in the very areas in which she generally displayed high intelligence, she now acted simple and dull.

When I called my client's attention to what she was doing, she was able to see the validity of my observations rather quickly. She gradually began to unfold the story of how she first came to play what some would describe as her "dumb blonde" role. She recalled that as a child she had been very competitive in spelling contests, arith-metic, and essay writing. She also enjoyed sports compe-tition, and she was very successful there, too.

Davis thought that perhaps a critical year for her came when she was a sophomore in high-school. She went out for the debate team, and in one of the contests she had crushed a male opponent. After the coach had heaped heavy praise on her, my client's parents took her home and sat her down for a long conversation. They pointed out that she was a beautiful girl and that one day she would make a wonderful wife and mother. Not the way she was going now, though, they warned.

"Boys don't like girls who beat them," said her mother. "That boy you beat tonight looked awfully hurt!"

Davis continued to hear comments like that from her parents all through high-school and college. They even fought about whether she should have a career or get married. Her parents, of course, wanted her to get married.

This client soon realized that to her parents being feminine meant being passive and looking up to men. They had taught her that women should be supportive of men, not compete with them.

I pointed out to her that she did not have to accept her parents' viewpoint. "You can do both—support and compete—at different times, Jan," I explained to her. "It's not a case of one or the other. You certainly support your husband, and yet you do some things better than he does. He doesn't fall apart; in fact he seems to welcome the challenge you offer him."

Davis recognized that she was afraid of "crushing the masculinity" of her male peers. She feared success because she felt that it would isolate her from men, and soon thereafter from women as well. So she unconsciously played a role to protect her from those consequences. She was saying, "Look at me. I'm pretty, feminine, and not as smart as you. I can't hurt you!"

Within a few weeks this client had worked through her conflict. She learned that men are not as fragile as she had thought, and that femininity and competency are not opposites. And I know that her rise within the business world reflected a reduction of fear of success and guilt over success.

●

Take a good look at the cost of success and what it's worth to you. Certainly there are difficult—perhaps painful—discoveries to be made about yourself. Yet the rewards are great. The battle lines are clearly drawn: It will either be self-mastery or self-defeat.

PHILLIP S. WEXLER

Phillip S. Wexler is president and co-founder of Ashtin Learning Systems, Inc., and co-author of the original "non-manipulative" selling program.

Phil received an Associate of Arts degree from Ocean County College in New Jersey and attended Monmouth College and the University of Pittsburgh.

Before his involvement with Ashtin Learning Systems, Phil spent ten years in the security industry. He began his career as a salesman and worked his way through many levels of marketing to become the national marketing director of a major security company, Marriott Security Systems.

Throughout this experience, Phil's major responsibilities centered on dealing with people. Whether in management sales or training, people skills were always the key. Phil's talent in interpersonal relationships has made him a highly respected speaker, trainer, lecturer, and business consultant.

His expertise has also earned him a long list of satisfied clients ranging from such firms as AT&T, Southern Bell, Continental Telephone, and Chrysler Corporation, to hundreds of local real estate and insurance companies throughout the country.

Phil has written several articles on selling for trade journals and marketing newsletters. Among them are "Removing Pressure and Still Getting the Sale," published in *California Real Estate* in 1977. He is also co-author of the recently published book *Non-manipulative Selling* (Courseware, 1979).

Phil lives in Atlanta, Georgia, with his wife Sue and his daughter Ashley.

You can contact Phillip Wexler by writing to 1145 Terramont Drive, Roswell, GA 30076 or Ashtin Learning Systems, Box 13135 Atlanta, GA 30376. Telephone (404) 993-5700.

IMAGE –
THE SILENT PERSUADER

by PHILLIP S. WEXLER

For many years now I have had the opportunity to go into colleges and universities all over the country and lecture students in the marketing departments. The first question I used to ask every group was "How many of you intend to become salespeople when you leave college?" Few people raised their hands, even though statistically more than half of them would be in direct-sales jobs, probably commissioned sales jobs, shortly after graduation. This concerned me a great deal; what that said to me was that they were settling for a sales job because they couldn't get into a profession of their choice.

Through these students, and later through salespeople in my training classes, I came to the conclusion that the public-at-large (and salespeople in particular) had a negative impression of sales. The word *professional* was tossed around a great deal but was rarely used in direct connection with selling. This bothered me; I pictured myself as a well-trained professional who was proud of being a salesman. I didn't mind people calling me a salesman. I had *salesman* written on my business card.

I decided the reason so many people had difficulty applying the word *professional* to sales was that no one had ever defined a sales professional.

I decided to try to define *professional image,* so as to set a goal that someone starting on a sales career could work toward.

In certain occupational fields all you have to do to be called a professional is have a certain job (doctor, lawyer, public accountant). The word does not necessarily imply competence. In other occupations, regardless of how competent you are nobody thinks of you as a professional.

I believe that professionalism has to do with how you perform the job rather than what the job is. Once I conducted a seminar in Victorville, California. I had never had an allergy before in my life, yet one morning during that seminar I woke up covered from head to toe with an itchy rash. It was a four-week seminar, with three-and-a-half weeks yet to go. I didn't have any idea of the cause, and in Victorville there aren't very many dermatologists.

When class ended Friday night I rented a car and drove to Los Angeles straight to UCLA Hospital Medical Center. After waiting about an hour in the lobby of the emergency room, I was finally led into a little cubicle. I put on one of those embarrassing backless gowns and waited there for about an hour.

At last a young woman walked in wearing a pair of jeans, sandals, a loose-fitting blouse only half-way buttoned, no bra, and a baggy smock.

A slightly askew name badge informed me that she was the doctor. Without speaking a dozen words to me, without once touching me or taking a test—no blood or urine sample—she just looked at me. She studied me for about five minutes. Then she wrote a prescription and told me that I could probably expect my rash to go away within a few days.

Well, the next day instead of hurrying off to the drugstore to fill the prescription, I called a dermatologist and made an appointment. This doctor was an expensive Beverly Hills specialist. He examined me for three full hours, took blood tests and urine samples and scrapings of the rash, looked at it under a microscope, and charged me $150. I took his prescription and compared it to the prescription that the young woman had written the night before—and much to my surprise *they had prescribed the same thing!*

Now I knew that in terms of competence, the UCLA physician was equal to the high-priced dermatologist. Yet I had not felt confident of her diagnosis. She didn't command my respect; she didn't build trust for me. She did not conform to the professional image I had expected in a physician.

•

Professional image involves many different elements. Some people give positive vibrations, some people give negative vibrations. Some people convey strong self-images, some weak. Just as some people project confidence, some project lack of confidence. We can talk all day about how unfair it is to judge a book by its cover, but that's what people do! People have very predictable responses to outside stimuli. It's an unusual person who can reveal genuine assets and skills once they have been obscured by an unfavorable initial impression. This is why personal image is so important.

By the way, if you think you will worry about your image after you're in a position of responsibility, think again! Here we are dealing with one of those chicken and egg stories—which came first, the chicken or the egg? Does a person become a professional because he or she *projects the professional image?* Or does a person begin to project a professional image because of *functioning in a professional capacity?* As you have probably guessed, I think I know the answer to that question.

The basic components of image, as we are going to define it, are: first impression, depth of knowledge, breadth of knowledge, enthusiasm, versatility, and sincerity. We will take each of these separately, detailing what it is, how you get it, and what the stumbling blocks will be. Let's start right away to build your professional image whether you are a salesman, a teacher, a plumber, or homemaker. Your goal is to be a *professional person.*

First Impressions

We've all heard the expression "First impressions are lasting impressions." We've all heard that you get only one chance to make a first impression—but have you ever given this serious thought? Have you ever considered how you come across to others? The impact of many a first meeting has prejudiced a relationship long after that initial impression was made. Days, weeks, months, even years later, it's possible to get a sale or lose a sale based on the way you projected yourself during a few crucial minutes.

Just what is a first impression? It's made up of many components. It involves dress, grooming, voice, handshake, eye-contact, body posture, your briefcase, your pen, your jewelry, and your car. Everything a person sees or experiences in connection with you during the very first moments of contact contributes to the impression you make. The way you choose to manipulate each of these factors decides how others will perceive you.

Positive first impressions make subsequent communication with others easy and comfortable. Negative first impressions can cut off a relationship before it even gets started. If I had to say that one facet of a professional image was more important than the others, I would choose first impression. You may never get a chance to show off your sincerity, your knowledge, or your enthusiasm, if the first impression you make is a poor one.

•

Have you ever judged another person's personality, competence, or honesty solely on the initial impression he made on you? What's the first thing that comes to your mind when you think about a person with a heavy Brooklyn or midwestern accent? What strikes you first about a person with a weak handshake, sloppy grooming, poor hygiene, bad vocabulary, poor posture, or ill-fitting clothing? And I'm sure you've met people who can be described in some of these ways—we very rarely meet people who can't make some improvement in the initial impressions they make.

A good friend of mine who was in graduate school had a difficult time landing a job. He interviewed for a number of university faculty positions, and although he was a brilliant student with unquestionable credentials and most people liked him, something always stood in his way. A particular department head took an interest in him, and although he did not offer my friend a job, he did him a valuable favor. He told my friend that his image was causing insurmountable problems for him in his interviews.

141

My friend asked me to help him with his image. I knew him as a warm, friendly, and helpful person. It was hard to look at him as an outsider. But when I did I noticed that his taste in clothing was atrocious. He wore obviously inexpensive and mismatched clothes—lots of polyester and plastic in indiscriminate combinations of stripes, plaids, and colors. His shoes were seldom polished. In addition, I saw that his hair looked greasy and his handshake seemed limp. Furthermore, he spoke in a low monotonous voice and maintained little eye-contact with others. His professional image was nothing more than poor, and in cherishing him as a friend I had never noticed that before. No wonder the faculty members wondered if he would fit in.

I tried to give my friend some helpful hints while telling him how much I respected him. I showed him how to improve some of the facets of his image, and believe it or not, after he reworked his image he was offered a position at the first university he applied to. It makes me sad to think about all the people along the way who never got to know my friend and appreciate him the way I do. But now he is making the best of his future.

•

Research has demonstrated that you can change people's responses to you by simply changing some aspect of your image. One easy thing to change is your handshake. What makes a good handshake? It should be strong and firm, but not overwhelming. (Don't be a bone-crusher. That creates as much negative impact as the dishrag handshake.) Don't hold the other person's hand too long. That becomes a violation of intimate space, as does the two-handed handshake. Step forward, make good eye-contact, grasp the other person's hand with yours, and shake firmly. That starts the relationship off on a good note.

Here's a note for dealing with the ladies. Classically, you shake a woman's hand when she offers it; if she doesn't—you don't. However, in the business world today I think it's becoming more acceptable to take a woman's hand without waiting for her to initiate. This is especially true when you greet one woman in a group of men. It is a slight to shake the men's hands and not automatically extend your hand to the woman. (If you are a saleswoman you can make it easier on your male clients by immediately offering your hand—they may be experiencing some tension in trying to decide what to do!)

Before you get the chance to shake someone's hand, they have observed how you sit and walk. Make sure your posture is positive. Avoid extremes. Don't walk with a strut, a shuffle, or a bounce. When you sit, sit straight and relaxed.

But the first thing anyone notices about you, long before the handshake, long before the walk and the posture, is *the way you're dressed.* Not enough can be said about personal hygiene, grooming, and dress.

•

Standards of good grooming and hygiene are commonly known, yet often ignored. How many people do you encounter in your organization with dirt under their fingernails or dandruff on their collar? How about female coworkers with too much hairspray or makeup? Have you ever spoken with people who breathed out a strong odor of tuna fish, garlic, or alcohol? Have you ever noticed that a co-worker has worn a particular shirt or suit once too often? And, most important, are *you* completely innocent of all of these grooming violations?

The way you dress makes a statement about you. Before you open your mouth to say who you are, people have judged you by your clothes. Clothes don't necessarily make the person, but they lead others to form lasting ideas about that person. When you get dressed in the morning, dress out of an intelligent choice. And if you're going to dress in a way that does not create the optimum advantage for you, let it be because *you made the conscious choice to do it,* not because you didn't know any better. (If you wear a green shirt with yellow pants and a blue jacket, let it be because these are your favorite colors—you know it's a terrible combination, but you love it, you're willing to pay the price, and you do it anyway!) Clothing is a powerful image-maker.

To project authority and success, dress in a conservative manner. Try to buy clothes made of natural fibers; although they will cost a little more initially, they will last longer and look better. This includes wool or cotton suits, cotton and silk shirts and blouses, silk ties and scarves, and leather shoes and belts.

Select low-key and classic colors, patterns, and styles. White, blues, and soft pastels are good for shirts and blouses. Effective colors for suits are all shades of gray and blue (except, for men, the very lightest blue) and beige. Conservative plaids, pinstripes, small herringbones, and tweeds are good choices for material. A less expensive suit that's properly tailored will look better than a poorly tailored expensive suit.

•

I must admit that I have seen people follow all of the above rules and still make a poor first impression because they didn't know how to put it all together. Learn how to combine your clothing. Use complementary colors. Your tie or scarf should pick up a color in your suit, shirt, or blouse. Men's socks should blend with their shoes and suit. And men: Always wear over-the-calf socks so your skin doesn't show when you sit down and cross your legs.

A long-sleeve shirt is recommended with a suit. Jewelry and accessories should be simple and functional. Scientific testing has proven that the authoritative image for women involves the use of a two-piece skirted suit with the same basic color patterns and colors as men's clothes.

If your height, weight, or age is creating an image problem for you, the correct clothing can alleviate it. There are books you can read and people who can explain it all to you.

Finally, your voice should be well modulated. Don't speak in a monotone. Your voice should be strong and full, but, like your handshake, not overwhelming.

Depth of Knowledge

The next component of image is depth of knowledge. Depth of knowledge is *how well you know your subject,* your particular area of expertise. That includes knowledge of your company, your industry, your competitors, your strengths and weaknesses relative to your competitors, good management—if you're in management—and good communications.

Do people come to you with questions about your company and industry, or do they go to someone else? Do they avoid you because you usually don't know the answers? Does your depth of knowledge project credibility and demand respect?

The more you know about your subject, the more professional you sound. Make every effort to learn as much as possible about your company, your industry, and your competitors. Learn the policies and the procedures within your company and your competition's. Know your product line, not just the products you are involved with but *all* your company's products. (You never know when a lateral transfer might be the stepping stone to your future.)

Study current situations and trends within your industry. Read trade journals and discover how you rate within the industry compared to your competitors. Take advantage of any training programs your company may offer. Whatever field you're in, develop the reputation of being the person who knows the answers.

Breadth of Knowledge

If depth of knowledge is how deeply and how well you know your field of expertise, breadth of knowledge is a passing acquaintance with all the subjects in the world. Do you know at least a little bit about a lot of subjects, so that you know enough to make an intelligent contribution to any conversation? How well can you converse with other people in *their* fields of interest? Who won the football game on Saturday? What are the latest developments in the Middle East?

Imagine two salesmen trying to get an appointment with the same purchasing agent. A purchasing agent's day involves a lot of time constraints. But it just so happens that this particular agent has a free hour today and two salesmen are out in the lobby and want to see him. One of them is an expert in his field, and no matter what you bring up, he brings the discussion right back to his own area of expertise. It's the one subject he can talk about. The other salesman gets fairly high grades in his own subject area and also has a broad scope of knowledge. It seems as if no matter what subject you bring up, he can get enthusiastically involved.

Now, assuming that both salesmen are selling a product of no immediate need to the purchasing agent, which of the two will get an opportunity to sell to this agent today? You can bet it's the second, the one the agent will feel most comfortable with.

People with a broad scope of knowledge make others feel relaxed—others think you're interested in the same things they are. That's the important difference between the salesman who is merely an order-taker, who gets an appointment only when the company needs his product, and a creative salesman, whom people will see just to be able to spend some time with him.

•

Unlike depth of knowledge, where your company shares the responsibility for educating you, breadth of knowledge falls solely on your shoulders. How do you expand your breadth of knowledge? Well, assuming that you read trade publications and other books in your area of expertise, you also must read a major city newspaper every single day of your life.

Now what should you read in the newspaper? When I ask that question in my seminars, some people say the sports section, some say the fashion page, some say the front page, some say the comics. It appears that most people read sections they're already most comfortable with. Unfortunately, that's not going to help their breadth of knowledge.

You need to read the newspaper from *cover to cover.* You might skip the classifieds and obituaries—I could forgive you that. But, especially in small towns, even the classifieds and obituaries are relevant to your success. You never know when one of your clients may experience a death in the family. Knowing that will be important in relating to him. If you live in a small town, be sure to read the local, as well as the metropolitan, paper.

You don't have to read every single word of the newspaper. Read each headline and the first few sentences of each story. If a story has special interest for you, finish it. But the *gist* of the story is all you're really looking for.

147

Find out what's happening throughout the world, as well. Read one of the major news weeklies—*Time, Newsweek, U.S. News & World Report*—on a regular basis. They summarize the major events in every facet of life from entertainment and people to the international scene. The weekly news magazine provides a perfect launching pad for a week's wide-ranging, informed, casual conversation.

•

If you're not reading books on a regular basis, begin right now to make it a habit. And another excellent way to expand your breadth of knowledge is to use non-productive time (I call it windshield time)—when you're driving the car, when you're watching yourself shave in the morning, doing your hair, or sitting in the bathtub—to listen to self-help audio-cassettes. Self-help cassettes are available on just about any subject you can think of. While you're getting ready to go to work, or are on the road, turn on your cassette player and broaden your knowledge.

Listen to the radio—be aware of the current music trends. Keep informed about current movies and theatrical events. If you've never been to a symphony orchestra performance, go hear one. All of these things will make you the kind of person people will want to be around.

One warning about this subject: If you don't know anything about a particular subject don't try to fake it. I remember once walking into a client's office and seeing right away that he was a motorcycle fanatic. The walls were covered with motorcycle pictures, and the room held a good many trophies.

I was only 19 at the time, and my boss had instructed me to always show an interest in the customer's interests. So I started talking about motorcycles and about how into motorcycles I was. The client looked at me and said, "Fantastic! I happen to have two bikes out back. Let's you and me go for a ride!" And I'd never been on a motorcycle in my life.

You can't fake it. If you can't genuinely contribute, then show interest by asking questions. You flatter the person by your show of interest, and you learn something about a new subject at the same time.

Versatility

The next area of image deals with a concept called versatility. We've all been brought up on the golden rule, "Do unto others as you would have them do unto you." Have you ever thought about whether that really works or not?

I am not a very time-disciplined person. I don't think much about time. Given my own inclinations, I sometimes arrive late, sometimes early. I rarely come on time. I don't use time efficiently. Take any job that somebody else would do in half a day, and it will probably take me all day—I'll get sidetracked and forget to pay attention to the clock.

Now if I treat other people the way I want to be treated, sure enough, sometimes I'll run across people who aren't time-disciplined, just like me, and they won't mind my lack of discipline at all. But just as certainly I'll come into contact with people who are very conscious of time, who use time efficiently and expect me to do the same.

Behavior versatility is the willingness and the skill to *adapt your style of behavior to the people around you.* I know people who are skillful at adapting their personalities but aren't willing to do so in most situations. Likewise, I know people who are willing in all situations but not very skillful. It takes both for adequate flexibility.

149

Then understanding and adjusting to other people's personalities helps build trust with the people around you.

Enthusiasm

In order to project a professional image to the people around you, you must evidence a deep-seated commitment to them, their company, their products, their customers, and the people they work with. That commitment is projected through *enthusiasm*.

For an example, think of your favorite entertainer. I'll use one of mine, Sammy Davis, Jr. Now no one can deny that he presents an enthusiastic image to his audience. Try to imagine that tonight in my home town of Atlanta, Sammy Davis, Jr. is going to play in a small club. In order to cover the cost there will be a high cover charge, $100 per couple. I decide that I like Sammy enough to pay $100 for a pair of tickets for my wife and me, so we go to the club and take our seats. Then we discover that the drinks are $10 each. Our total investment at this point is $120.

Before long there is fanfare at the front of the stage and out comes Sammy. Now I know that when he makes his appearance he's going to be the same effervescent Sammy Davis that we expected. He's going to sing the 12 or 14 songs that his contract calls for, and there will be conversation with the audience, jokes, jive, scat singing, and tap dancing besides. I know I won't be cheated.

I remember seeing Sammy Davis once, a long time ago, when he had just climbed out of a sick bed with pneumonia and left the hospital against doctor's orders. That night he had more enthusiasm than a lot of entertainers have at their healthiest. He's a professional—he's consistent. He knows how to give the level of energy and enthusiasm that will make me feel good about my investment. (Everyone in the audience that night turned to the person next to him and said "There's a professional!")

•

My best advice to any person in business, whatever the level or the job, is if you get up in the morning and you can't muster up the enthusiasm to get you through the day, stay home. You'll lose more credibility, you'll lose more potential for the future, by being unenthusiastic than you'll ever lose by staying home.

Now, what if that happens with any regularity? If you see yourself here, change jobs—you're in the wrong business! How often is regular? Everybody has a bad day. I'm sure that there are days when you wake up less enthusiastic than you would like to be. Even on the worst days, within 20 or 30 minutes you should be able to bring that level of enthusiasm up to get you through the day. The exceptions should come only once or twice a year.

Zig Ziglar always refers to today as being a *great day.* There's always one thing that you can count on for making today a great day. And that's the fact that *you are here to experience it!* What do you have to be enthusiastic about? Yourself, your company, your family, your peers, your superiors, your subordinates, the people around you! They all should contribute to your enthusiasm.

There's no excuse for inadequate performance. If you had paid to see a performer who was unenthusiastic because he'd just had a fight with his wife, would knowing the reason make you *feel* any better? If he gave his dozen songs and called it quits, because he'd had a few too many that afternoon, would knowing that make you feel any better? If you learned he'd just discovered that his business manager had been mishandling his money, would that make you feel OK about his lukewarm performance?

Those are the same daily excuses that managers across the country get from their employees when they point out: "Hey, George, you're dragging a bit this morning!"

"Oh, I've got financial problems."

"I had a fight with my old lady this morning."

"Boy, did I ever tie one on last night!"

We hear these kinds of excuses every day. They just don't make it. They are the mark of the mediocre, not the professional.

The professional has problems, too, but he rises above them. When he walks into his office, when he walks into a client's business, when he interrelates with his co-workers, he buries his problems. He puts them behind him and works at getting out of them.

The only thing you owe the rest of the world is to be enthusiastic about sharing. Most managers like to see enthusiasm in their employees, and the enthusiastic worker seems to work harder, longer, and more accurately than others. You can infect other people with your enthusiasm. Likewise, if you're not enthusiastic, neither are the people around you.

Sincerity

Sincerity is the last aspect of your professional image. This is the easiest one to describe. I can describe it in one sentence—four words. *You can't fake it.* As in the other areas we have discussed, there has to be conscious commitment, not just because I told you so, but because it works. Your sincerity or lack of it is quickly projected to everybody around you. If you come across as insincere, it will be more damaging and it will have more adverse effects on your relationships than if you disregarded any of the other components.

Make a concentrated effort to improve your professional image in its six aspects. As with any change of behavior, when you initially do it, it may be uncomfortable. But if you do it long enough it will become a part of you.

•

All the things we have just discussed require an investment on your part. A big investment. The need to make a favorable impression may require that you dress in a manner you might not have ordinarily chosen. It may cause you to dress differently than your peer group. Yet versatility of style, the ability to be flexible, can be a great asset in establishing contact with the people around you. In so doing you create an atmosphere of *acceptance* of others, of validation. In this way you reduce tensions which might otherwise surface.

Similarly, you need to invest time in keeping abreast of developments in your industry. That time constitutes hours that you could spend with your family or at entertainment or recreation. Expanding your depth and breadth of knowledge requires spending time in areas that you are less interested in at the expense of things you are very interested in.

What's the payoff for this sacrifice? You determine that. The payoff will be directly proportionate to your investment. And no one ever got a return on an investment until he *made* that investment. Take the first step now!

VIRGINIA LEE

Virginia Lee is a speaker for civic, social, school, and church organizations. She gives specialized programs and success seminars that incorporate the educational and inspirational aspects of alignment, expansion, expression, energy, and enthusiasm.

"To live dynamically and courageously," says Virginia, "to be creative and productive, you must know where your energy comes from and how to sustain and direct it."

Virginia is a lecturer and teacher for the John Robert Powers personal development programs. She is also an author, poet, and musician—she plays piano and organ and sings lead in the Mission Viejo Chapter of Sweet Adelines women's barbershop chorus. She is the mother of four children.

In 1978 she received her Bachelor of Science degree at California State University at Fullerton and initiated and administered a pre-school program in the city of Orange.

Virginia participated in the Silent Unity Prayer Ministry at Unity Village, Missouri, where she has been tour-guide director and was invited to be retreat coordinator. She is certificated by the University of Science and Philosophy, founded by Walter and Lao Russell, and is also trained in public relations procedures, publicity, and copy writing.

Virginia is the author of *Universally Yours* and *Lovingly, Me*, volumes of prose and poetry. Her third book will be *Life Is Like That*, a collection of short analogies with practical insights.

You can reach Virginia Lee by writing 26828 Salazar Drive, Mission Viejo, CA 92691; or telephone (714) 770-2822.

THE TRIUMPHANT TRIO: COURAGE, CREATIVITY, CHANGE

by VIRGINIA LEE

TODAY

Ragged edges?
    Jagged seams?
Life's passed by you?
    Lost your dreams?

Courage up,
    Head held high,
Know that daring's
    Worth a try.

Start today,
    Do what you can.
Plan your life,
    And live your plan.

Life proceeds
  Its self-planned way,
If you do best
  What you do today.

Change is ever with us. The seasons, the tides, day and night, the weather—they all attest to the inevitability of change as part of life. Most of us can handle predictable, forseeable changes. But how to cope with changes that we appear to have no control over, changes that are thrust upon us? My poem "Today" addresses feelings that we all experience from time to time.

If we are sincere about self-development we meet change by continuing to reprogram our thoughts, feelings, and actions so that we feel good about ourselves and the people in our lives. But we still seem to fight it. We try too hard to avoid it. We don't *want* to look for a new job, or a new mate, or new friends. We don't *want* to move. Sometimes we don't *want* to figure out how to make more money, even when we desperately need it.

Change produces stress, we are told, and most of us have barely enough energy to function adequately in the life we're living right now. How can we possibly handle more change, more stress?

The Gut Level

Stress is something that hits right in the solar plexus, in the pit of your stomach, commonly termed "at the gut level." When it hits you hard, you know your life is changing. There is an immediate impact on the nervous system, with a feeling of heaviness and exhaustion. Stress is an extreme expenditure of energy at all levels within the body, mind, and emotions. Your thoughts are shattered by a multitude of *ifs*, *ands*, and *buts*. Doubt and fear take over.

We are all acquainted with the stress that comes with divorce, moving one's home, or losing one's job. But did you know that *success* also produces stress? Success produces stress because it, also, requires the expenditure of unaccustomed amounts of energy. Success may drain our energy reserves by bringing lack of privacy, frequent interruption by telephone calls, disruption of meals and sleep, and loss of quiet time.

Learn to recognize stress and call it correctly, so as to prevent misnaming it as fear, anger, disease, doubt, or sin. Stress is inevitable.

If change produces stress, the reverse is also true: *Stress produces change.* I want to impress this upon you, because once you have realized this fact, *you are in charge of your life.* Once you realize that stress is bound to occur, but that you are in charge—once you become consciously responsible for the happenings in your life—you have ceased to be a victim.

As a young couple, my husband and I never seemed to have enough money. We decided to limit our family to four children, instead of going on to the six we had originally planned, but the money just didn't seem to catch up. And so when our last baby was just eight months old I found it necessary to go to work. I had been a public school teacher before my children were born, so I signed up to do substitute teaching.

How I resisted having to work! I especially disliked the hassle of trying to get a babysitter when I was called at seven in the morning. I did it, but I didn't like it. I behaved like a victim of circumstance, under stress but coping.

Then a dramatic thing happened. I met a man named James Blackwell. This man was able to lead people through a reverie of thinking and feeling, while experiencing what they are feeling. He knew how to ask questions that reveal the real basis for their experiences.

I told Jim what was happening in my life. As I spoke aloud what I was thinking and feeling about my job, as I discussed the pictures in my mind, it became evident to me that I was actually setting up my life so I *had* to work! I liked all the sympathy and attention I was getting: "Oh, Virginia, I don't see how you manage to do all that with those four children!"

As Jim worked with me I discovered that I really *liked* working. I enjoyed getting dressed up, putting on my makeup, and getting "out." I enjoyed the stimulation of other people.

My work was important to me! When I looked back at all the energy I had expended to avoid doing something I liked, I was amazed. How much easier it became when I *took charge* of what I was doing. I was overjoyed with my new outlook and all the energy available to me.

First You Must Be

Stress produces change. I want to repeat this over and over, because once we have accepted this turn-around in our thinking, life becomes dynamic and forward-moving. On my business cards is printed this affirmation: "I am aligned with the upward, forward energy of life. I am creative, courageous, and successful."

I'm sure that at times it was stress that caused me to become aligned with that upward, forward energy of life. It was stress that pushed, pulled, and shoved me into the dynamic life flow.

It takes courage to experience stress, to allow change to happen, and to devote your energy to it. Creativity is an important part of this package. If you do not anticipate great things in your life and in yourself, you will not get them.

Living should not be "coping." Living should be dynamic and free and full of productivity and satisfaction. When you realize that stress is bound to occur, but that you are in charge, you have seized upon a fact of life: Stress, proclaimed as a dynamic, positive, motivating force, can *become the catalyst* for your creativity and productivity. When you have decided to use stress as a catalyst for change, you will have new enthusiasm. Being in control over your life brings a certain sense of power to replace helplessness, and that generates its own energy. And that energy becomes enthusiasm.

When you take control over your own life and are enthusiastic about what you are doing, your enthusiasm and creativity, in turn, produce positive changes. It's amazing how our "outer" worlds change when we change the way we respond to each situation, each point of stress.

One of the prerequisites for creativity in living is the following: *Consciousness precedes demonstration.* You must *be* within the deepest part of your thinking and feeling, and consequently *act out* what it is you really want in life. You must *become* your affirmation. In *Wells of Abundance,* E. V. Ingraham puts it this way: "I am filled with the wisdom, love, power, and substance of God; and as an irresistible magnet, I draw to me all that is needful for my most complete expression in life." This is the Law of Attraction. *What you are, you attract to you.*

A famous star was hit by a scaffold and was knocked out on stage when she was rehearsing for Muni Opera in St. Louis, Missouri in the early '70s. A friend of mine noticed that when the singer was interviewed on television, she had repeatedly remarked "That just *knocks me out!*"

Our words have power! It's imperative that we be careful of what we say. It's just as important to be careful of what we *are.* The words we speak will eventually manifest themselves, and so will the feelings that live in the deepest levels of our being. What we say and what we are must agree. Being at odds with ourselves produces increased stress, and we must be of one accord if what we desire and plan is to come about.

Teachable, but Not Changeable

How futile to go to all the trouble of dressing to look one's very best and then, on receiving compliments, to say "Oh no—I really feel I must look quite awful!"

I attended the 29th reunion of my high-school band. I knew that life had been fairly good to me and that I looked infinitely better than when everyone had last seen me, 29 years before. However, when they said how great I looked, do you know what I said? "Yep, I finally lost my baby fat!" (How I wished I had just smiled and said, "Why, thank you!")

I'm a student of metaphysics, and I find it essential to keep up with what's happening. It's good to continually think and study and grow. One of the things I often wondered about was the Biblical phrase "blaspheming the Holy Spirit." I had heard various interpretations and was not entirely satisfied with any one of them.

During my graduate studies I asked one of my professors which interpretation he believed to be correct. Dr. McLaren was an ordained Presbyterian minister. I was impressed to discover that he had done a three-year study on this subject. He concluded that in all religions to blaspheme the Holy Spirit meant to be unteachable.

I was truly intrigued. We are all either growing or dying. A person who is unteachable remains static and inert, like a plant without light and water. Something within dies, and eventually so does the body. To be *unteachable* is to give up one's life.

Now I want to make the distinction between being *teachable* and being *changeable*. Of course we want to be able to change, but let's not confuse that with being *changeable*: Webster gives this definition of *changeable*: liable to change; subject to alteration; fickle, inconstant; mutable; variable; as a person of *changeable* mind. Synonyms for *changeable* are: *fickle, inconsistent, mutable, uncertain, unstable, unsteady, variable, wavering,* and *whimsical.*

When we become teachable, and when we adopt the ability to grow and to change, we must not become changeable. We must not be uncertain or wavering; we must set goals and strive steadfastly toward them. We must not be afraid of changing our goals when we have reached them, or when they are no longer functional, but we must operate with a certain *consistency,* even when we are creatively changing.

There are times when we simply *allow* perfect creativity. There are times when we merely *consent* to change, and creativity happens naturally. We frequently set goals and then insist that they be attained in a specific manner. But setting goals can be compared to making a shopping list—the goals aren't all-inclusive or absolute. We must always be receptive to new ideas as they present themselves, just as we are receptive to buying fresh foods in season or sale items, even though they may not be written on our list.

Consider the palm tree that bends in the high winds of the hurricane. It does not break like the oak tree which we so commonly epitomize as the symbol of strength. Rather, the palm tree bends and gives with the force of the wind. When the storm is over, the palm tree returns to its former upright state. Life is like the storm, and it requires of us that we give way and change before it.

Acting As If

Abraham Maslow's theories on self-actualization have been of great interest to me. I recently came across a book by William F. O'Neill, *Selected Educational Heresies,* which states that the process of growth, of "peeling away inhibitions and constraints" to become oneself is "unlearned, created, and released" behavior rather than acquired behavior, expressive rather than coping.

People who are self-actualized are prompted by "growth motivation," and are therefore creative in their approach to life. Other people are "deficiency motivated" and continually seek to satisfy their unmet needs. Deficiency-motivated people must have other people around. Growth-motivated people are relatively independent of the physical and social environment; their development and creativity depend solely on their own potential and latent resources.

One of the most efficient methods of releasing our latent resources, once we discover what they are, is "acting as if." This exercise requires a great deal of insight into our own needs for growth, as well as the courage to initiate the change. The prerequisite is a desire for change and a teachable nature.

"Acting as if" demands that you put aside any limitations on your previous thinking and feeling and step into the role of whatever you wish to become. Practice on strangers, who won't perceive any difference in your behavior.

One of my friends teases me about talking too much, so I decided to try to be more quiet. Practicing this new role requires me to put out a good deal of energy—but it's fun. (However, when I am feeling truly quiet, my friend is thrown off guard. He finds it a strain to do the talking!)

We get so used to the roles we play that sometimes

we resist change even when we *want* to change. We have to make a conscious effort. Change is full of risks, and risk is fearful, but it allows us to experience how the universe works. By working through your fears you can learn to *master the world.* Conversely, if you avoid risk and allow yourself to be run by fear, the world—the environment and other people—will control you.

One way we can enter into risk wisely is by using our power of imagination. We can "walk through" in our minds the things that we are contemplating changing.

Learn to act out your changes in your mind. (This is especially useful if you have been uncomfortable with "acting as if"—act as if in your mind. Do it first in your imagination, and when it becomes easy, then do it in real life.) Just as you have a walk-through when you are buying a house and the escrow is about to close, you can have a walk-through before you incorporate something new in your life.

In child development it is called *adding to the repertoire* when the child sequentially develops new abilities and capabilities. This same term is used by musicians as they learn new pieces, memorize them, and include them in their performances. Adding to the repertoire is a very valid way of describing what you do as you change creatively. You are constantly adding to your personal skills repertoire.

Be sure you have learned the number well, memorize it until it is easy to play, and then perform it! It really isn't hard to do once you catch onto the sequence of events that take place first *within you* and then *in your outer world.*

Creativity Follows

Always remember that consciousness precedes demonstration. Once courage has created change, true creativity follows. This means that whatever your specialty, it cannot come forth until you operate from the standpoint of growth-motivation.

Reading and writing prose and poetry have always been a great source of satisfaction and joy in my life. But when I have experienced periods of great need, the creativity stops. At those times all my energy goes into merely maintaining.

Life proceeds from glory to glory. We must see life as this and recognize stress and change as good in order to benefit from the process.

You are always forming and reforming, either consciously or unconsciously. Your life is what you create in your imagination. To live dynamically and courageously, to be creative and productive, you must know where your energy comes from and how to sustain and direct it.

Success lies in knowing *who* you are, *what* you are doing, and *why* you are doing it. The *how* is stimulated and generated by the expectation of accomplishing the first five. Courage and creativity await your expresssion of them; change is the catalyst which completes the Triumphant Trio!

KATHLEEN L. HAWKINS, M.A.

Kathleen Hawkins is a novelist, a public speaker, a prize-winning poet, and a speed reading consultant.

Ms. Hawkins is a reading specialist with master's degrees in reading education from Eastern Michigan University and creative writing from San Francisco State University. She has twelve years' teaching experience, from elementary school through adult education. She has taught public speaking, oral and written communications, and remedial reading; and for the past five years she has specialized in speed reading.

She is a speed reading instructor with National Management Institute in San Francisco and a speaker with Dible Management Development Seminars. In her intensive one-day reading courses, she shares ways to dramatically increase your memory and gives strategies for smuggling reading time into a busy schedule.

"I find it ironic that it takes me *months to write* a novel and only *minutes to read* one!" Ms. Hawkins laughs. "But after I teach you to speed read, you're welcome to speed read everything I write. I have total confidence that speed readers get all they need out of their reading with excellent comprehension and enjoyment as well."

Speed reading has been a valuable tool for Ms. Hawkins in her work because writers have to be avid readers. Her articles and books span a wide variety of subjects: physics, time management, memory, learning strategies, metaphysics, brain phenomena, reading, and business management. Her research takes her to many departments in the library: science, literature, psychology, business, and education.

Her young adult novel, *The Garbage and the Flowers*, is being considered for publication. You may look for her speed reading book, *Beyond Speed Reading*, sometime next year.

You can contact Kathleen Hawkins by writing to 860 26th Avenue, San Francisco, CA 94121; or telephone (415) 386-8806.

STRATEGIES
FOR SPEED READING

by KATHLEEN L. HAWKINS, M.A.

If you don't have time to read this, you need to!

I don't have to convince you that in your lifetime you will read millions of words which come to you via newspapers, personal letters, magazines, journals, technical reports, office memoranda, books, brochures, and catalogs. If you're like most people who find their way to my seminars, you need strategies to allow you to read more in less time.

Relax! The Speed Reading System is here! It will increase your reading speed the minute you apply it. And you will begin to read more intelligently with better comprehension than ever before.

171

The Speed Reading System is a set of skills which evolve out of three natural functions of your brain:

1. Response to motion
2. Receptivity
3. Closure

RESPONSE TO MOTION

People have an automatic response to motion, probably based upon early survival instincts.

Imagine for a moment that you are an early cave dweller crouched next to a crackling fire near the mouth of your home. Out of the corner of your eye you see something move.

You better believe you're going to look! It could be a saber-toothed tiger doing his grocery shopping in your neighborhood; you could be on his list right next to the mammoth steak.

Back to the present, if you're having a crucial conversation with someone and another person walks into the room, chances are good you'll glance up before resuming your important meeting. It's a throwback to that old survival instinct.

As a speed reader, you will capitalize on this automatic response to motion by using your moving hand to guide your eyes smoothly down the page. Because your eyes follow the downward motion of your hand, they are pulled down the page faster than your normal reading rate. The following examples further explain the principle of motion as it relates to reading.

Page-Glance Preview Motion

The first of two hand motions you will use for speed reading is the page-glance preview motion, a sweeping preview technique which enables you to expand your focus, accustom yourself to greater speeds, and prime your mind for what is to come.

With your hand in a relaxed position, palm up or down depending upon which is most comfortable for you, sweep your hand down the middle of the page in a question mark motion. Do not go all the way to either margin, but stop about one-quarter inch short of the print on each side. *(See Figure 1.)*

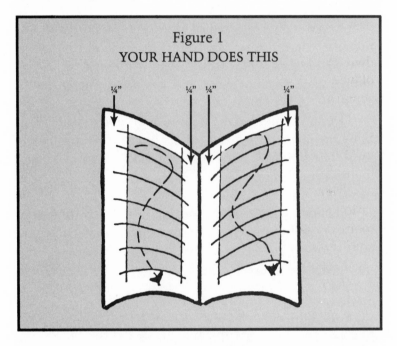

Figure 1
YOUR HAND DOES THIS

Allow the movement of your hand to guide your eyes smoothly down the pages. Do not force your eyes to follow your hand exactly, but rather, let them drift back and forth down the pages, picking up names, places, characters, and colors.

Remember, page-glancing is a *preview* technique, so you won't be reading *per se.*

Expand your focus. A speed reading student once told me, "Speed reading has greatly expanded my field of vision. I realize it especially when I'm driving and find myself taking in the license number on the car in front of me at the same time I'm noticing that the guy in the car next to me needs a shave!"

Speed reading expands your awareness both visually and psychologically. You become more receptive to the overall picture, to the *themes* of your reading, rather than to each single word.

The sweeping motion of the page-glance technique programs you to loosen up your thinking and to look for the main ideas in your reading. And you may find, as you practice page-glancing, that you are beginning to revise your focus in everyday life.

Take a moment right now to look about you. What does your focus encompass? This book? The immediate room? The building across the street?

How much more there is to the world than just your immediate surroundings!

Consider your outlook on life. Do you allow your focus to become obsessed with routine details? Or do you allow yourself to see the whole picture, set some long-range goals for yourself, and think about the meaning of your life?

Accustom yourself to greater speeds. Have you ever driven a car for a long time and glanced at the speedometer to see that it had inched dangerously upward since you last noticed? You had become so used to a particular speed that what originally seemed fast now seemed slow.

In the same way, after page-glancing for a while, your brain will become comfortably used to faster speeds. Returning to word-by-word reading will seem like a snail's pace.

Prime your mind. Are you familiar with the old-fashioned pumps on wells? On the farm you couldn't just go out and pump the water up—you first had to *prime* the pump by pouring a cupful of water down it. This would start the water flowing. Page-glancing is a little like pouring a cupful of words into your mind to get the ideas flowing.

Page-Glancing Practice

Now put into practice what you've learned about page-glancing. Select a fairly easy novel. Do not choose short stories or technical material at first.

Since you are retraining your eyes and mind to read in a new way, make sure the print in your novel is easy on the eyes and not too small. Place a bookmark in the middle of your practice book and page-glance from the beginning of the book to the marker. Page-glance any blank pages as well, so as not to break your rhythm.

When you reach the marker, return to the beginning. Page-glance through again, all the time questioning yourself: What is this book about? Who are the characters? What ideas can I pick up before going back into the material and reading it?

During these previewing drills, allow yourself about three or four seconds a page.

You may notice that when you first begin working with this technique you see more words on either the right or the left pages, or the tops or the bottoms of pages. Several whole pages may fly by without your noticing anything at all. Don't worry about this—it's perfectly normal.

Throughout the week, continue to practice your page-glancing in other books. Smooth out your technique by making a point of noticing something in every paragraph.

As you become more comfortable with your page-glancing preview techniques, you will start to relax and gain confidence. And you will pick up more and more information.

RECEPTIVITY

The second natural tendency of your brain which helps you speed read is *receptivity*. Receptivity is the ability and the capacity to receive ideas and impressions.

It is the natural state of your brain to be perceptually and psychologically receptive. In fact, when you were a baby, your only job was to receive impressions from the outside world—and to delight the grownups while doing so!

Every impression you received influenced you and structured your future behavior. And gradually (if you are like most people) your life became cluttered with many unnecessary judgments and habits.

In speed reading, to be perceptually receptive means to expand your focus and not let it contract on the page. It means to relax—don't frown or squint—and to move your hand smoothly down the page, allowing the ideas to flow into your mind.

Psychologically, being receptive means being ready to experience speed reading itself, as well as being open to the ideas in your reading. You can accomplish this by re-serving judgments and by being objective and willing to learn.

How You Learned to Read

Your attitudes about reading go way back. Imagine for a moment that you are in first grade.

You are sitting on a little wooden chair in a circle

around a teacher. The room is filled with the murmurs of other children and the smells of paint and chalk and maybe wet woolen mittens drying on a heater.

You're reading from a little booklet. The teacher is having each child read out loud to determine how he decodes words and where he needs more help.

Okay so far—except that you're probably equating reading with *talking,* since in that early reading group the two are the same.

You are also taught how to unlock words by looking at the parts, by studying the vowels and the consonant blends. This continues throughout the first grade. Sometime later your teacher instructs, "Now button your lips and just *think* the words instead of saying them." However, by this time you are probably fixed in the habit of inner speech, or subvocalization.

The habit of subvocalization slows the reading process. By saying every word to yourself, you are asking your brain to slow down to keep pace with your saying the words. Instead, speed up your reading to keep pace with your thinking. Your brain takes in information automatically.

When you subvocalize, the words go from your eyes to your ears, and then to your brain. When you speed read, words bypass your hearing mechanism and go directly to the brain. You can get a sense of this by choosing a passage in this book and by making a gentle hissing sound under your breath as you read silently. Notice the absence of words in your mind. If you are still hearing some words, practice this exercise some more. Move your eyes along the lines faster and phase out the words.

You may find some comfort in knowing that many good speed readers still subvocalize somewhat, but they have reduced it to saying only a few key words and ideas as they move rapidly down the pages looking for meaning.

A Demonstration

Cut a dime-size hole in an 8½ × 11 sheet of paper. Open a magazine, and, without looking, place the paper over a picture so that only a small portion of it can be seen through the hole.

Try to explain the picture as you move the sheet across the page, revealing only a small portion at a time. You will be forced to focus on one spot at a time, as word-by-word readers do. Your conscious mind is involved, with deliberate concentration, as you try to logically piece together whole ideas from details. This laborious process significantly impedes comprehension.

Now remove the sheet of paper and view the entire picture. Your understanding will be more complete as you relate the parts to the larger picture. Removing the paper and viewing the whole picture is analogous to speed reading.

Suspend Judgment

Speed reading reverses your approach to reading. You learned to read from part to whole; dealing first with sounds, then words. In speed reading you deal first with the *whole*, by understanding the ideas in your reading, and only then do you fill in the details.

I ask that you suspend your judgment and have fun with the page-glancing technique. After years of being a speed reader, I still enjoy practicing my page-glancing drills. It's a good mental tune-up.

CLOSURE

The third function of your brain which helps you speed read is closure. Closure is the tendency of the brain to complete a message, as in a figure, letter, word, or paragraph, given minimal details.

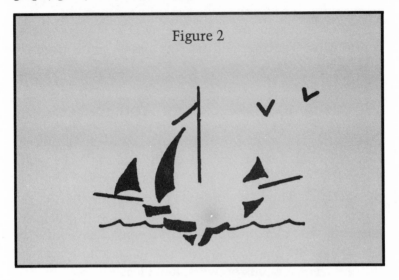

Figure 2

Look at Figure 2. Can you identify this object?

You probably said it was a sailboat or ship. But look again—it's nothing but a few triangles and straight lines. Your brain was so hungry for the whole picture that it automatically filled it in.

> N—w —s th— t—m— t— m—st—r y—-r
>
> r—-d—ng s— —t w—n't m—st—r y—-.

You probably have no trouble filling in the blanks to complete the message.

In each of the above cases, your mind made sense out of a few details. You did not always have the ability to do this. When you were very young and saw your first sailboat, you had to work to figure it out: What was that thing? How did it run? What was it used for?

The same was true when you encountered your first words. You had to learn each letter of the alphabet and its respective sound. You had to learn that words stood for the communication of thoughts. There were many things to consider in order to make sense out of reading.

Now that you are older, seeing is no longer such a complicated venture, and reading has become largely a memory process.

How to Make Closure Work for You

From now on, after you have previewed a section by page-glancing, read it by searching out *only the main ideas*. If you must subvocalize, say only the key words in the material. The key words are often the nouns (people, places, and things) and the verbs (action words). All meaning will cluster around these words. Say only the key words and know that your brain sees and registers the connective words between key ideas.

The brushing technique. The brushing reading technique is a tighter hand motion than the sweeping page-glances which are used for previewing. Brushing is used for filling in the details after you have grasped the big picture and the main ideas.

Smoothly underline every sentence until you become comfortable with the technique, then brush under every three or four lines of print. *(See Figure 3.)*

Brush to within one-quarter inch of the margins on each side. Use three fingers instead of one. (If you point as you read, you may have a tendency to focus on one word at a time.)

Practice with brushing. Practice the brushing technique a few moments in your practice book.

Mark off 20 pages. Page-glance through the section twice, looking for ideas. Then read the section with the brushing reading technique, looking for key words. It doesn't matter that you have already practiced in the same book. Right now you're trying to get a feel for the style of reading fast. Allow yourself about 10 to 12 seconds a page.

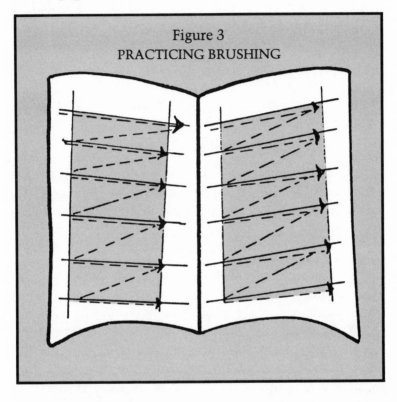

Figure 3
PRACTICING BRUSHING

Then mark off the next consecutive 20 pages. Again, page-glance the section to get a preview, then read it using your brushing reading technique.

Continue like this throughout the book. Be sure to rest your eyes *before* they become tired, about every 20 pages during practice reads, and every 10 pages during regular reading.

An excellent technique for relaxing your eyes is called *far focus*. To rest your eyes, simply switch your focus from the page to a distant point out the window or across the room. Breathe deeply two or three times, blink comfortably (never stare for any reason), and reflect on what you have just read. Then resume reading.

APPLYING THE SPEED READING SYSTEM

The speed reading system uses three steps which are based upon motion, receptivity, and closure.

1. *Preview the section you are going to read.* Use the page-glance preview technique. Get an overall picture of what is going to be in that section.

2. *Read the section.* Use the brushing reading technique to fill in the ideas you picked up in your preview. Look for the key words and know that your mind sees and registers the connecting words as easily as it completed the picture of the sailboat.

3. *Postview the section.* Tie in any loose ends by postviewing the material using your page-glance technique again.

Your brain automatically condenses information. Recall a recent conversation you had with a friend. Do you remember it word-for-word from the very beginning, or do you remember the general ideas and the moods it evoked?

When you tell a friend about a movie you've seen, don't you automatically condense the story into plot and themes, rather than giving a detailed, word-by-word account?

And yet, when some people read, they insist on focusing on each separate word with a fierce perfectionism that not only isn't necessary, but actually hampers your brain in its search for understanding.

It is not a matter of life or death for you to read and remember that some character in the book is wearing blue shoes! And at any rate, if such information is crucial to the story, any decent writer will make a point of it more than once.

A Good Way to Test Your Comprehension

How can you determine how well you are understanding the material you read by this method?

A good way to evaluate your comprehension is to discuss each of the topics in the table of contents, index, or glossary. Reviewing them for a friend (whether imaginary or real) is an excellent way for you to evaluate where your strengths and weaknesses lie.

You can also ask yourself whether you have satisfied your purpose in reading the material. Did you read the book to be entertained, to gain information, to learn a new skill, or to improve yourself?

You will remember what you read longer if you *do something* with what you have learned. Give a report, discuss it, meditate on the ideas, illustrate it, or make a movie of it!

Two Hints for Reading Technical Material

Technical material can be approached differently from stories and novels. You still preview and read with a purpose, so that certain facts attract your attention. However, with technical reading you obtain the greatest benefits from *changing the order* of your reading.

Last things first. Always read summaries and conclusions first, then prefaces and introductions. Then glance through any charts, graphs, or pictures. This may be all you need to do to get what you need from the material. If you need to, then glance back through the main body of material for additional supporting evidence and examples.

Use checkpoints. Using a soft-lead pencil, make checks in the margin next to unfamiliar words so you can look them up later if they are not explained in the text as you continue to read. Also mark the passages you want to study more carefully later. When you've learned the material, you can easily erase the checks.

Add the Personal Factor

Goethe once said, "The writer only begins a book. The reader finishes it."

In other words, a book means little unless it is read. You, the reader, bring a personal dimension to the story, the elements of your own memories and experiences. A book is a little like a conversation. You can respond with your attention and appreciation. Then you may share the story with others.

Likewise, information is not half as important as your relationship to the information. By themselves, facts are nothing. For example, Halley's comet, which measures three miles across, passes Earth once every 76.1 years. These two facts would mean little to you unless you were a scientist planning to launch a probe through the comet, or unless you were going to be in the vicinity and wanted to watch as it passed through the morning sky. Therefore, target your *purpose* for reading and select material that will enrich your life.

Writers everywhere are waiting for you to finish their books, to apply their techniques, to enjoy the stories they have to tell, and to share your new knowledge and insights with others.

Full speed ahead!

MICHAEL R. SIMONEK

According to Michael Simonek, there are two types of people in this world, talkers and doers. Michael tries to encourage everyone to be an active participant in life, to become a "doer."

He joined the "real world" himself during his last year in college, when he received a sales job offer which he just couldn't refuse. After four years he was responsible for accounts totalling annual sales of more than $1,000,000. He invested heavily and experienced remarkable success with real estate, stocks, commodities, and a business he bought and resold. He also began working with a small non-denominational church, where he still speaks and counsels regularly on a volunteer basis.

Although not rich in the sense of being a millionaire,

Michael does have enough financial security to allow him to pursue the three *R*s—reading, writing, and racquetball. Among his other prominent interests are philosophy, free market economics, and sports. He is involved with several writing projects, and thanks to a Dible Management Development seminar, he soon will be starting his own publishing company. He is also testing some experimental marketing techniques through his newly-formed San Miquel Sales Company. As you can probably guess, Michael's favorite words are "Let's do it!"

You may contact Michael Simonek by writing to 348 Via El Chico, Redondo Beach, CA 90277; or telephone (213) 375-5941.

INNER SECRETS OF SUCCESS

by MICHAEL R. SIMONEK

A college law professor walked into his introductory law class the first day of school and said, "If you want to be a lawyer then you had better learn to think and speak like a lawyer. I can only teach you the law. It's up to you to become a lawyer."

Any profession you enter, whether it be law or real estate, insurance, or accounting, requires you to think in terms of that profession and speak its language. That is equally true of motivation and success: If you want to be a motivated and successful person, you must learn to think and speak *in the way motivated and successful people think and speak.*

Your thoughts and your words go hand-in-hand. Your words are the outpouring of your thoughts. New thoughts can change your words. New words can help change your thoughts. And ultimately, as has been said before, if you want to change your life, then change your thoughts.

It is easy to motivate people for success. There are many good books and stories. There are also many good speakers. But what happens when you finish the book or leave the magical aura of a good speaker? How long do you stay "up?" How long do you stay motivated in the face of worldly opposition? How long does that feeling last—one week, one day, five minutes? Do you then fall back to your same old self, less motivated and less successful than you want to be?

If you want to be successful each day of your life, then you must be motivated *from within yourself.* You are going to have to think and speak motivation and success. Once you achieve motivation from within, you won't need a motivational fix every month or so.

Through correct thinking you can realize any success you desire. Just like the Datsun commercial, *you will be driven!* But first, you must retrain and reconstruct your thought processes.

Your mind is like a computer. You have probably heard the buzz word GIGO (Garbage In, Garbage Out). The same principle applies to the human mind. You can produce—think, speak, solve problems, and live—only to the limits of the information in your mental storage bank.

If you program a computer with "one plus one equals zero," then no matter how you do the calculations, one plus one will always give the same incorrect result. Similarly, if a child is told that no matter how hard he works he will always be poor, chances are he will work himself to the poorhouse.

We all react to life the way we are programmed to

react. We get out of life what we are programmed to achieve. When you recognize this you will realize how programmed, and in many cases how trapped, people really are.

However, the human mind differs from a computer in that *we can control* the information that is put into our memory banks. We can also review what bits of data and information we have stored, and if we find them incorrect or out-dated, we can replace them with current data. That is just what we are going to do in this chapter. We are going to review some of the information you have stored in your mind and give you the opportunity to replace it with better ideas.

Are you programmed to be a success? Let's look at some areas in which you may be falling short.

Be Responsible

If you were to view the lives of many successful people you would find that a single silver thread runs through each of their lives. That silver thread is responsibility. Successful people choose to be fully responsible for their lives. They recognize that in order to achieve success they must captain their own ships; they must chart their own courses and accept the destinations reached. They may believe in fate or luck to some small degree, but more important, they recognize the power of the individual *to create his own luck* by actively responding to opportunity.

Responsible people are not excuse-makers. When the chips are down they know there is no one to blame but themselves. Responsible people assume the full weight and consequence of their actions. A pro football player was recently interviewed on television after being injured in a freak accident. Even though his future career was jeopardized by the injury, he didn't blame bad luck or misfortune. He simply said "That's one of the risks of playing the game." He was acknowledging that the decision to play football, with all its inherent risks, was one he had willingly made.

When you take full responsibility for your life, any success and happiness you achieve *is all yours*. Accordingly, the intensity of the experience is much greater. By the same token, events entailing pain, heartache, and sorrow are equally intense. But these are the risks of playing the game. We accept them willingly—responsible people recognize that life is a two-way street.

Some people wonder how they can take full responsibility for their lives while acknowledging the greater force in the universe, which most of us call *God*. It is important to realize there is no conflict between taking full responsibility for your life and having spiritual or religious beliefs. God helps those who help themselves.

If you sit on your hands, so to speak, you are like broken-down machinery in a factory, poor tribute to your Creator. By building full responsibility into your life you can begin to function near your intended potential. If you acknowledge the force of God in your life at the same time, God will work through you as you work.

Inspect and analyze the data you have stored in your brain regarding responsibility. If you find any information that is not consistent with a new responsible you, *eliminate it from your memory bank.*

Examine the way you react to the world. Do you make excuses? Do you blame your misfortune on bad luck? Consider how you rationalize occurrences in your life. Pay attention to your speech; your words will give you information about your automatic response patterns.

If you were late for work, how would you respond to people who question you about it?

- "The traffic was heavy."
- "The weather was bad."
- "My alarm didn't go off."

These are all responses indicating lack of responsibility. Responses which demonstrate responsibility might be:

- "I didn't get up early enough to beat the traffic."
- "I didn't allow time for the bad weather."
- "I forgot to set my alarm clock."

You should recognize that no one succeeds in passing off an excuse. Excuses are clothed in some kind of invisible aura which is immediately detectable.

Excuses do nothing to better your position. If, as in the case above, you are late to work, excuses will not change the fact that you were late. But they may damage your credibility by demonstrating to your boss that you lack responsibility. If, on the other hand, you take responsibility for being late, you may improve your credibility and your image at the same time. Make lemonade out of your lemons!

Responsibility will drive you to better yourself. Start adding it to your life and find out how much better you feel.

Develop a Good Self-Image

The biggest battle some people will ever have to fight is that of overcoming their upbringing. It is through our upbringing that we develop our self-image and its related counterpart, self-esteem. To a large degree, self-image and self-esteem come mainly from our parents and secondarily from social and economic class, neighborhood, race, religion, or any number of other external psychological or physical influences.

People who grew up during the depression years and were taught to be thrifty were probably financially devastated by the effects of inflation, which favors high consumption and credit. People raised in low economic classes are sometimes programmed for lifelong poverty. They make their life choices in a way that will guarantee following in their fathers' footsteps. Some people go through their lives believing they are inescapably dumb because that was drilled into them as a child.

What messages molded your self-image? Uncover them and change them. Take time right now to reflect on your self-image and how it was formed. Do you find negative messages coming back to haunt you? Do you recognize any of your behavior patterns as a product of limiting messages?

Don't be too critical of parents and friends as you review your past. At any one time, people do the best they can with what they've got. Acknowledge the conditions you grew up under, but tell yourself that they are part of your past, *not your future.* Erase them by turning your attention to new positive thoughts; or turn them into positives by changing your perspective. Remember that your childhood, both the good and the bad, helped build your character. Each and every experience you've had has been valuable.

Free yourself from all mental hindrances. You are, from this day forward, *a new person totally free of any negative shadows cast by your upbringing.* You must have a positive self-image to be successful. If you don't have one, get one. Start today!

Reject Limitations

There are no limitations! It's as simple as that. Don't you think people would understand that by now? I mean, for heaven's sake, we put a man *on the moon* years ago!

I accept absolutely no limitations from myself or other people, and that includes all handicaps. (Actually, there is one limitation that I acknowledge. That is mental retardation so severe as to prevent the individual from comprehending or communicating. And even in those cases I don't limit God.)

The limitations most people allow to rule their lives are nothing but demonstrations of their lack of responsibility and maturity. Many people have a hang-up about money. They feel they never have enough money to do what they want. Arnold Missner, a man I used to work for and respect very much, once said "Money is the cheapest commodity."

At first that was hard for me to accept, but in a few days I began to see he was right. It's true. Money *is* the cheapest commodity. It is knowledge and experience that are so costly and so valuable.

A lady once told me she wanted to travel. "Fine," I said, "why don't you?"

Her answer, as you can probably guess, was "No money."

I will not accept "no money" as a valid answer, but lack of money could be a significant factor, depending on the type of travel you wanted to do. If you wanted to travel in order to stay in luxury hotels, eat at the finest restaurants, and otherwise go first class all the way, then yes, you *might* need money—but I am sure it would be possible to find ways around it.

However, if you wanted to travel to expand your horizons, to see new lands and new people, and to experience all the color and variety the world has to offer—then I would tell you *"You do not need to have money."*

Absurd, you say? Not at all. Airline hosts and service personnel travel for pennies. I know someone who works for the railroad, and another person who works on luxury cruise ships, and I am sure there are many other ways to obtain significant travel benefits and even get paid while you travel—*if you really want to do it.*

Do you want to buy a house but find that you can't qualify for a loan? You don't have to let lack of income stop you. I bought two houses at the same time when technically I couldn't qualify for even one. Before that I bought a business and got 100 percent financing!

There are no limitations except the ones you accept. Obviously, NASA didn't accept any preconceived limitations about putting a man on the moon. They just went out and did it. Sure, it took them a long time to do it, but they did it—and that's all that counts! You are limited *only if you allow yourself* to be limited.

Do you live by the word *can't? Can't* is some people's favorite word. It is the biggest roadblock in life. If you say you can't, *there is no possible way you can!* It's as simple as that. If you want to be a successful person, you must eliminate negative thoughts from your mind and negative words from your vocabulary. Never forget that thoughts and words go hand-in-hand.

If you pay close attention, you will find that when people say they can't, they really mean *they don't want to.* If someone says he "can't" play the piano, sing, dance, paint, or go to school, he really means that he doesn't want to. He doesn't want to spend the time, work, practice or money to achieve his "desire."

Eliminate all negative thoughts and language. Don't say you're too short, too fat, too old, or too dumb. It's not true—you're just right!

Remember that many, many people have overcome poverty, illness, physical and mental handicaps, and lack of education to achieve success. The library is full of their stories. There is the marathon runner who has no feet, the artist who has no arms, and the entertainer with cerebral palsy.

Countless immigrants entered this country without a dime in their pockets or a word of English in their vocabulary—yet they went on to achieve their success. *There are no limitations.* Anything you say that limits your ability to achieve and become is just an excuse. The greatest natural resource on earth is man's *unlimited potential.*

Establish Goals

Many of you, by the very act of reading this chapter, are seeking success—or more of it. Success is simply attaining your goals. Much of society interprets success as money, more specifically, megabucks! But money doesn't necessarily have anything to do with success, although it seems to cloud many issues.

It is possible to have your success mean money. If you are a salesperson, you may set a sales goal of $1,000,000. Or you may have a goal of accumulating $1,000,000 in your bank account. As a company president, you may be striving to obtain a profit projection. However, it is important to realize that money is usually *a means to an end.*

Your million-dollar sales goal is a means toward company growth and investment. Your million-dollar bank account is a means toward your self-actualization.

On the other hand, you may have a goal of running five miles. You may establish a goal of visiting all the countries in Europe. There are infinite goals and subsequent successes not tied to money. Many people simply have a goal of being happy, and their success will be the smiles on their faces.

In dealing with goals there are two things to consid-

197

er; first, selecting the goal and second, a method by which to achieve that goal.

What are your goals? If you hesitate and stammer, then you have not carefully defined them. Your mind is a goal-oriented device. Given a clear picture and understanding of the desired object, the mind proceeds diligently to secure it. However, if the goal is confused or out of focus, there is little the mind can do but wait until the fog lifts.

In some cases people lack clear or definite goals because they are afraid to commit themselves. They can't decide. They're not sure if they really want that something or not; or they fear being trapped into seeking a goal that somehow becomes obsolete in this rapidly changing world. Don't worry about that! You can adjust or change your goals as you go—that's OK. But you have to start heading in *some* direction.

Be aware of the difference between interim goals and ultimate goals. You may have a goal of building a million-dollar bank account so you can retire from the 8-to-5 business world. Is your goal, then, one million dollars? Yes and no. The monetary goal is really just the means to another goal, retirement.

Chances are you could retire on much less money. But unless you kept the ultimate goal in mind you would just keep on working for that million.

There are many methods of setting goals. Some methods use writing, others use pictures, some use visualization, and others involve a form of meditation. Whatever you do, find a system that works for you. Personally, I like to use meditation and visualize the successful achievement of my goals. Also, I write each goal on a separate piece of orange paper and tack it up on the wall across from my desk.

There are also many methods for achieving goals,

and again, I have a favorite to recommend. I use the buddy system, and it is much like it sounds. Pick a friend or a family member with whom you have similar interests and can communicate well. You report your progress to your buddy at regular intervals, perhaps biweekly or monthly, and your buddy offers support, motivation, and even rewards.

Attaining goals requires work and time. The bigger the goal, the more work and time it takes to achieve it. And the higher the goal, the greater the satisfaction when you reach it.

My old friend Jeremiah had some things to say about goals. He said, "Set your goals high, very high, and then take satisfaction in your progress. The progress is what's important, and it will help motivate and drive you to your goal. Also, see time as your friend in achieving your goals, not as an enemy to fight against."

Finally, attaining goals always requires some sacrifice. It's important to maintain a balance between sacrificing today for tomorrow's goals and living a full life each day. There's no point in sacrificing everything to achieve some future goal, because tomorrow you may not be around. It's unfortunate, but we don't often get a 30-day notice from the Big Boss telling us our contract on Earth is up.

However, what good would it be to live life to the fullest each day, sacrifice nothing for future benefit, and end up sixty or seventy years old with little or nothing achieved? The key, then, is balance. Live each day to the fullest *with a bit of sacrifice* for future benefit—and find fulfillment in sacrificing a bit each day. Take satisfaction in your progress and your daily life will become more rewarding.

Learn From Failure

As you review the information in your mental data bank, there are two areas of failure you should consider. The first area concerns setting oneself up to fail, and the other concerns fear of failure.

It may sound strange, but some people actually do set themselves up to fail. Some people feel comfortable in a failure mode. It's most likely due to response patterns that have been programmed into their brains from childhood. (Did you always lose to your friend, brother, or sister? Were you given sympathy or attention as a child when you lost rather than won? Did your parents or your coach tell you "We don't expect you to win?" This can be programming for failure.)

The second area of concern is *fear of failure*. Do you fear failure? If so, why? Do you fear losing the love of friends or family if you fail to achieve your goal? Or do you fear embarrassment or ridicule? If these fears are valid, you might consider that negative people can adversely affect your performance. Do what you can to separate yourself from them, or, in the case of family, try to teach them to be positive and supportive.

Now I would like to tell you something that will help you if you have any hang-ups about failure. Throughout my life *I have never failed or had a bad experience!* This is not to say that everything I have attempted has been a success, or that I haven't had a few rough times. However, the events of your life will appear eminently more pleasurable and fulfilling from the right perspective: There is no failure in life, because *we learn* from all our experiences, and learning is the most important thing in life.

Remember what we said about money being the cheapest commodity? Knowledge and experience are certainly far more valuable and powerful. For this reason, the greatest success in life is to gain knowledge and experience. And you do that mostly by working toward your goals. Remember what Jeremiah said: "Set your goals high and take satisfaction in your progress."

A few years ago I talked to a man in the real estate business who made a big impact on my thinking. He had spent ten years building a vast fortune in real estate and was about to put it all into one somewhat risky project. I expressed my concern and asked what would happen if he failed. His response was inspiring: "My boy, it took me ten years to build my first fortune. To build it all over again would take me only three years." The real products of his success were obviously his knowledge and experience.

Each experience, good or bad, is a stepping stone to greater understanding. Life is one constant lesson, a progression of experiences designed to enlighten and season your soul. It is all good, and it is all positive.

Recognize Opportunity

When dealing with opportunity you must first understand where it comes from. Simply put, *change creates opportunity*. If it were not for change—the birth, growth and death cycles, the evolution of man, and the many other functions of change—all life and existence would be frozen like a block of ice. There would be no such thing as time, either, for time is just a way of gauging relative distance between events.

Thank God for change! However, many people fear it. In a very simplistic analysis, I think that is because they look backward instead of forward. They look back on what they had, fearing to lose it, rather than forward to what they might have in the future.

Since our world changes daily—even by the minute—there are new opportunities every day. Overpopulation in one area may create an opportunity for high-rise construction. Growing medical costs have created opportunities for doctors who believe in alternative forms of health care. The gasoline shortage created opportunities for the small car. The birth of a son or daughter may give you a new chance to find fulfillment in life. The death of a family member may bring new opportunities to understand living.

There is nothing you can do about change. Change is going to happen whether you like it or not! So look upon it as your friend and listen for opportunity to knock. It is up to you to recognize it and use it to your benefit.

Develop Inner Security

I'd hate to upset you if you happen to be security-oriented but it's important to tell you that *there is no security in this world!* Security, in the popular sense of the word, is a trap perpetuated by banks, life insurance companies, and false teachings. Wars, freeways, earthquakes, and no-fault divorce end all traditional ideas of security.

Everything is going to be different tomorrow or next year, so don't get yourself too comfortable! The only possible form of security exists in three things: your spiritual beliefs, the inevitability of change and new opportunities, and the realization that all you've got is yourself. Everything else could be here today, gone tomorrow.

Consider what things give you a feeling of security: a large bank account, a large family, close friends, a home paid for free-and-clear? Recognize that by some freak occurrence they could all be taken from you tomorrow. Be especially aware that no job is secure.

If you seek security develop your spiritual beliefs,

develop positive attitudes toward life, and most important, develop yourself! The only security lies in being able to deal with the world as it changes day by day, in charting your own course through life. The ultimate security lies within yourself.

Enjoy Your Work

On a wall near where I live are some worthwhile graffiti: My favorite is: "Pleasure is a motivation in itself." Do you wake up in the morning hardly able to wait to begin your day? How often do you work through the night on some brilliant idea you just thought of to help your job?

On the other hand, perhaps you hide when the morning alarm goes off or have nightmares about your job. Have you ever prayed that some night an earthquake would level the building you work in? Could it be there is no satisfaction, no pleasure in your work? What good is work if it gives you no pleasure? What good is your *life* if your work does not give you pleasure?

Webster's Student Dictionary tells us that *pleasure* can mean any or all of the following: "Delight, enjoyment, will, wish, or choice," (as in "What's your pleasure?"). All these meanings are very pleasant ones.

We find that *work* means: "Toil, labor, employment, task, duty, product of toil or labor." Also, anything accomplished: "A deed, a feat." Webster goes on to differentiate work from labor, toil and drudgery. *Work* is a general term for effort that has a useful purpose. *Labor* commonly implies more strenuous exertion. *Toil* is painful or fatiguing labor. *Drudgery* is especially dull, irksome, and distasteful work.

Now I submit to you that what I do is *work*, and what many people of this world do is *labor, toil,* or *drudgery.* Furthermore, what I do is work because it is useful and gives me pleasure and is my choice.

Now wouldn't you like to enjoy your work as I do mine? You can, *if you want to.* You may not be able to do it overnight—in fact, it took me five years to achieve the financial independence I needed to do my own thing. But you can do it.

If you set any goals at all for your life, please make it your objective to find work or attain a position that will give you pleasure.

Take Action

Now it's up to you! I have given you ideas and words of successful people so that you can think and speak as successful people do. I can teach you success, but *it's up to you* to become successful!

Take action! I don't know who said it, but "All glory comes from daring to begin." Take the first step, even if it's a small one. You can increase your stride as you progress.

Your potential is unlimited, so let your mind and spirit soar. No story is greater than that of human spirits driven by will and desire to overcome obstacles and achieve their goals. Make that your story, too.

JACK CLARKE, Ph.D.

Dr. Jack Clarke is a psychologist in independent practice in Reno, Nevada. He is also director of the Counseling and Testing Center at the University of Nevada at Reno. His professional certifications include: Certified Psychologist, State of Nevada; Certified Marriage and Family Therapist, State of Nevada; Registry in the National Register of Health Service Providers in Psychology; and Certified School Psychologist, State of Nevada.

He holds a Bachelor of Arts from the University of Redlands, Redlands, California; a Master of Science from the University of Oregon; and a Doctor of Philosophy in counseling and personnel work from Arizona State University. He continues to expand his education by looking for practical aspects of the theories of psychology and neuropsychology.

Dr. Clarke has had a wide variety of work experiences. He has been an executive for the Boy Scouts of America and has taught at every educational level, from elementary through graduate school. This broad background has given Dr. Clarke an overall view of human development from early childhood through the adult years and into retirement.

Dr. Clarke has always been active in community activities and professional organizations. He has been a member of Kiwanis, Rotary, and ·Junior Chamber of Commerce. He has been active in his church and has served as a board member of the Center of Religional Life in Reno, Nevada, and the California-Nevada Conference of the United Methodist Church. In 1980 he was elected national treasurer of the Association of Counselor Educators and Supervisors.

He draws on his broad base of professional and community activities in presenting his workshops and speeches.

Dr. Clarke is listed in Marquis's *Who's Who in the West*, in the 1976 through 1980 editions, and in *Notable Americans of the Bicentennial Era*, published by the American Biographical Institute.

Dr. Clarke may be reached through his office at 100 West Grove, Suite 250, Reno, NV 89509. Telephone (702) 323-1027 or (702) 853-2956 (evenings).

CREATE-MATES: A MODEL FOR NEW MALE-FEMALE RELATIONSHIPS

by JACK CLARKE, Ph.D.

In my marriage-and-family counseling practice I often help couples update their marriage contracts. They're usually unaware that such a contract ever existed between them, but with every marriage there is a contract. A couple marries with certain expectations for the relationship. That mutual understanding constitutes a contract.

After a few years of marriage a change in circumstances, such as having a child, may change the relationship so that all of a sudden their contract no longer works. The new conditions require a reassessment of wants, needs, roles, and expectations.

A similar situation exists within the work force today. We are operating under antiquated contracts between men and women. Half of all family units have two wage earners, yet our society is based on the concept of one breadwinner and one supporting homemaker per family. In addition, the entire male-female working relationship is based on the outdated concept of supervisor-supervisee, with the female being the supervisee.

Changing Life Roles

For a number of years Professor Alexander Astin of UCLA has been conducting surveys of college students. His research shows dramatic changes in women's perception of their life roles. In 1970, 47.8 percent of the freshmen women surveyed believed that married women should restrict their activities and energies to the area of home and family. In 1975 that response was given by only 28.3 percent, and one out of every six women entering college planned to enter a career in business, engineering, law, or medicine.

Now these very women are finding their career progress blocked or slowed because of what I as a psychologist see as the lack of an appropriate relationship model. They are being prevented from progressing into equal jobs with men in percentages appropriate to their number in the work force.

Just as the married couple needed to update their contract, we need to update our society's contracts between working men and women. The current contract of the male being the supervisor and the female being the supervisee no longer works.

In the distant past one's career was usually chosen by heredity. If you were male and your father was a carpenter, you grew up to be a carpenter. If you were male and your father was a potter, you grew up to be a potter. Of course most women grew up to manage a household. But with the industrial revolution came a change in the career concept for men. A whole range of careers developed, and for the first time men were able to choose careers that met their personality needs.

Women did not make this quantum jump into industrial society. Women continued to be restricted to very few careers outside the home: teaching, nursing, secretarial work, and religious callings. And these careers more often than not did not match their individual personalities; women continued to stumble into, or be more or less forced into, their means of livelihood.

So we had a society in which men could choose from some 40,000 jobs and women could choose from less than a dozen, with only an illusion of choice involved.

Increased Psychological Sharing

When we subsequently mixed this work force, it resulted in men and women working side-by-side but well separated by status, interest, and financial reward.

Men went to work partly to enjoy the company of other men, with whom they had a common bond. Not only did they share job interests, but more than likely they also shared recreational interests. (All occupational career theory is based on a personality-need structure; the questions asked in helping a person select a career deal not only with the type work that the person likes to do, but also the person's recreational activities and cultural interests.)

Women entered the work force like as not out of the *sole* need of earning money. More often than not they did not share the after-hours interests of their fellow (male) employees. It was an expected result of their isolation that women would become the supervised, while men continued to promote men to supervisory positions.

Now women are considering their potential in all 40,000 occupations. A friend of mine is a pilot, and told me how he encountered a female voice from the control tower one day. He had requested landing instructions, and after repeating them back to the tower he said from force of habit, "Thank you, sir."

The response from the controller was "You're welcome, madam." He quickly got the point.

Now that women are freer to choose careers based on their interests and personality needs, we are moving into an era where men and women are going to be working together on a *quality* basis. Not only will they share work interests, but they will also share recreational and cultural activities. We can predict that men and women with like personality structures, needs, and interests will have a significantly higher percentage of attraction for each other than in the old system.

Love in the Office

A colleague and I have developed a model for male-female working relations. Dr. Kessler and I have each used this model in therapy, and it has been helpful to many people. The Create-Mate model enables men and women who work together to deal with increased physical and psychological closeness in a constructive and productive manner.

Men and women have much to offer each other in a career setting, and as a psychologist I firmly believe that we can have close personal friendships with the opposite sex without involving sexual expression and endangering primary relationships. You can use this model to enrich your work environment regardless of whether you are male or female.

The legendary office affair is an example of dealing

212

with uncomfortable closeness in a destructive way. Other destructive coping mechanisms are sexual jokes, innuendoes, and harassment. These problem behaviors spring from a need to express the perceived intimacy in the work situation. Constructive solutions are based on the realization that intimacy can assume various forms, and does not necessarily have to involve sexual expression.

Consider that the word *love* has many meanings. I love my wife. I love my dog. I love God. I love this cheese soufflé. I love my children. I love my job. I love to play tennis. Obviously, I'm not talking about the same type of feeling in each of these cases.

In conceptualizing our Create-Mate model we considered the four words for love in the language of the Ancient Greeks. These words, *epithymia, eros, philia,* and *agape,* effectively express the different elements of love. There is probably a blending of these four different kinds of love in every healthy relationship between human beings.

Epithymia

This word represents that element of love that is sexual desire. Obviously epithymia is a very important part of a marriage relationship. It should be a part of every loving relationship that we physically act upon. Epithymia may also enter into the working relationship; it's unrealistic to expect you will have no sexual feeling for someone with whom you work closely.

In the context of a work relationship, it is proper to contain this element of love, not to act on it. Many women have told me about losing their jobs because of sexual involvement in the office, although in all the years I've been a therapist I've never once heard a man say he lost his job because he was sexually involved with a female employee.

To help us understand epithymia in more detail let's look at another word, *affection,* as opposed to sexuality. Often couples will share with me the fact that they don't feel they can be affectionate with each other without the obligation to have sexual intercourse before the day is out. This is more than a trivial problem, because affection is an important part of one's psychological support system. The couple who can physically touch—hug, kiss, hold hands—without feeling a sexual obligation has many more options for expressing their love and caring for each other.

This is also true in the working environment. An expression of affection is important to sustain the working relationship. And men and women can express affection for one another in the office *if there is an understanding that this is not going to lead to sexual action.*

The prohibition on sexual action is the key. Men have always operated with this understanding in their working relationships with other men. We see it in sports every weekend on television. Most of us remember the open display of affection when our 1980 Olympic ice hockey team won the gold medal. Men and women need to be able to work through the issue of intimacy in a shared work situation in a similar way.

Here are some practical guidelines for handling and containing epithymia in a work situation. First, *verbalize your feelings and state the limits you feel are appropriate and necessary.* Second, *any form of sexual come-on is out.* This includes the wearing of clothing that is intended to communicate sexually, as well as sexual jokes or double-entendres.

Men and women need to assume equal responsibility for containing sexual feelings. The old model of the male being aggressive and the female saying *no* is no longer appropriate.

Eros

The term *eros* has taken on a sexual connotation in contemporary society, but the Ancient Greeks did not use it in that way. They saw eros as the kind of love that urged mankind toward higher forms of being. It was that element of love that was expressed creatively in drama, architecture, and art.

Eros is related to the excitement people experience when they solve a difficult problem or find an effective solution to a problem. It's that element of intimacy that allows two people to jointly create more than they could individually.

I have a friend who conducts a symphony orchestra. I have watched him be a good conductor of other symphonies and I have seen him experience the excitement that the orchestra, audience, and he himself generate during a performance. Just as this shared creativity results in superb music, the excitement of eros can always be used to stimulate productivity and quality, especially in the working environment.

Philia

The third aspect, *philia,* is friendship. It's psychological and emotional intimacy. Men in business usually attach themselves to a mentor, someone older and experienced who can help guide them in their chosen career. Philia is the type of friendship that would develop between a mentor and a protegé.

Philia can also develop between a man and a woman in a job environment. In fact, a woman entering any career field would be wise to find herself a mentor, as men have always done. (And even though women are beginning to assume their rightful place in the corporate structure, chances are the already-successful model will be male.)

Philia is that element of love you need not be afraid of. As most friendships grow they consume less time than in initial stages. The reason for this is the build-up of trust levels. In an established friendship it is unnecessary to spend a lot of time and energy maintaining the relationship. The time you spend with the other person becomes productive rather than developmental. Close friends make minimal demands on each other.

Agape

The fourth aspect of love, *agape*, was described by the Greeks as the type of love that God has for man. It's the kind of love that puts the other person's interests and needs before your own, so that you would never harm the other person in any way. It's the element of love in a working relationship where the Create-Mates wouldn't think of doing anything that would endanger or threaten either of their marriage relationships. Actually, it's the agape element of love that makes the other three kinds of love possible.

Making It Work

The Create-Mate model (see illustration) shows you how the four kinds of love can be blended into a variety of individual contracts appropriate to each situation. In the marriage relationship, all four elements of love have unlimited potential. There need not be any restrictions on expressing love to your spouse. Children, on the other hand, need affection from their parents without any suggestion of epithymia.

CREATE-MATE MODEL

	SPOUSE	CHILDREN	WORK ASSOCIATE	CREATE-MATE
EPITHYMIA	xxx	xx	x	xx
EROS	xxx	xxx	x	xxx
PHILIA	xxx	xxx	x	xxx
AGAPE	xxx	xxx	x	xxx

xxx = *Unlimited potential* / xx = *Defined limits* / x = *Unexplored*

In working relationships we can use the Create-Mate model to maintain a close relationship and keep that relationship in perspective. Here again, there will be defined limits on the expression of *epithymia*, with unlimited expression of other kinds of love.

The "Work Associate" column in the diagram represents work relationships that have not been dealt with in terms of the "Create-Mate" model. These relationships do not have existing contracts and can either grow into positive, healthy, productive relationships or develop in the opposite direction.

In adopting the concept of the Create-Mate model for male-female working relationships, there are some areas of caution. New relationships are always more exciting than old ones. Remember that. At home the neurosurgeon has to take out the garbage; at work we are likely to be doing those things we enjoy most, with few tasks we *don't* like to do. This can create an imbalance between the work relationship and the home relationship.

You also need to be aware of time limitations. The goal of new contracts between men and women in the work force is, necessarily, to allow for *more* productivity, not less. The relationship should permit individuals to realize more of their potential without interfering with the achievement of their goals.

The third potential problem area is that of trying to meet the deficiency needs of your spousal relationship through your on-the-job relationships. A colleague of mine was upset one day because her husband was going to go skiing with his secretary. She couldn't understand her jealousy. She told me, "I couldn't go—I have to work. So why shouldn't he go and enjoy himself? This isn't like me—I'm really not a jealous person."

I asked her, "When was the last time you and your husband went skiing together or had some other kind of fun?"

After she thought for awhile she understood her jealousy. Her husband was meeting his recreational needs with another female, instead of with her.

This is what I mean by deficiency needs. You will have more freedom within the work relationship if your spousal relationship is in balance. I recently read a book called *The Longest War*. It dealt with research on the male-female relationship. I hope that we are maturing as individuals to the point of ending that war.

Hopefully, the Create-Mate model will give you a tool which you can use to enrich your relationships with other human beings.

In addition, I hope that this model will help to create a healthy working environment for yourself and the people who work with you.

ALAN G.
ZUKERMAN, Ph.D.

Alan G. Zukerman, Ph.D., is a practicing psychologist and a management consultant. He spends most of his time helping others to get themselves and their goals together and providing the motivation and follow-through necessary to complete the job. In his spare time Alan dabbles in real estate and writes.

Alan earned his B.A. from the University of California at Berkeley in 1968 and his Ph.D. from the University of North Carolina at Greensboro in 1974. He is currently a licensed practicing psychologist in the State of North Carolina and is acting as the Director of Psychological Services at a state facility in the Commonwealth of Virginia. Alan speaks to both professional and nonprofessional audiences on a wide variety of topics.

Alan entered college at the age of sixteen, graduated from Berkeley in the tumultuous '60s at the age of twenty, and completed a book less than a year after getting his doctorate, while working full-time. Yet he describes himself as one of the world's laziest people, and he is proud of it.

How has he managed to accomplish all that he has done in his own life, plus helping others to be equally productive, while working in settings ranging from carwashes and factories to high-powered business complexes? Why does he think of himself as a lazy person? "It's all pretty easy," he says. "The key is to motivate yourself to get off your backside and take care of business. If you know how to motivate yourself and how to keep yourself going until you reach a target, you're going to have plenty of time left over to sit around and enjoy being lazy."

You can contact Alan Zukerman by writing 242 Temple Way, Vallejo, CA 94590; or telephone (804) 797-1348 evenings or weekends.

HELP FOR PROCRASTINATORS

by ALAN G. ZUKERMAN, Ph.D.

One of the easiest and most common bad habits to fall into is procrastination. Virtually everyone delays doing something sooner or later in life. Putting off going to the dentist, studying, doing that job report, cleaning the house, taking up that new interest or hobby, making repairs—the list could go on and on. The purpose of this chapter is to make you get up off your backside and do it!

Naturally, there is no guarantee; dedicated procrastinators will always find ways to delay getting into motion! However, these suggestions are bound to help, if you want to be helped.

WHAT MAKES US PROCRASTINATE?

I don't put too much stock in theories about originating

causes. They tend to be irrelevant to the problem at hand. In the case of procrastination, however, the link between the reasons why a person begins to procrastinate in the first place and what can be done to get things going is readily apparent.

We put things off when they are unpleasant. Who wants to take out the garbage or clean up the mess? What kind of fun is that? Who wants to memorize formulas or read about the Crimean Wars? It's not much fun to spend your day off fixing a sink or repairing a door. And when was the last time you had a ball at the dentist's? It's very easy to put off doing dull or unpleasant things, especially if there's no sword dangling over your neck.

We put things off when there are more appealing things to do. Why wax the car when you can get a golf date by simply picking up the phone? Why study when your friend is listening to good music with drink in hand? Why wash the dishes when a favorite TV show is coming on? We tend to select the more appealing choices.

We put things off because we are afraid. You put off asking your fantasy person for a date because you're afraid of being rejected. You don't tackle that big report because you're afraid you can't pull it off. You don't go to the doctor to check out those strange pains because you're afraid of what he or she might tell you. Fear of failure is a powerful cause of procrastination.

Fear of succeeding also enters in sometimes: What if I try to do it, find that I can, but don't like it after all? Some people will point to those who were famous and apparently successful, but obviously unhappy: "Howard Hughes was one of the wealthiest people in the world, and look how *he* died."

Plain fear can also be a factor. An employee may not

approach his boss for a raise because of fear of being put in the doghouse or fired.

We put things off because the payoff is too far away. Writing up that report could bring you all kinds of goodies once it's done, but that's three months off, and meanwhile the amount of work necessary to do the job looks mountainous. Or you need a job, but that involves looking, finding transportation, getting clothes, and lots of general effort and hassle. And there's no guarantee of when your efforts might pay off. You'd like the basement to be available for use, but it would take weeks of work to get it that way.

WAYS TO
COMBAT PROCRASTINATION

Any instance of procrastination could involve one or more of the delay-causing factors we have mentioned. In the presence of one or more of these factors, how does one *ever* get into action? Moreover, how does one move faster than a speeding bullet, with more energy than a speed freak and all the compulsion of a person who counts cracks in the sidewalk? There is actually a whole range of tactics effective in combating procrastination. They are collectively known as *contingency management*, the arranging of your circumstances to promote getting the desired things done.

You are controlled to a large extent by the circumstances of your life. The hours of your job, the distance to work, the ages of your children, your interests, your dislikes, your friends, your salary, your leisure-time activities—the list could go on and on. All these things can be called *contingencies* affecting your behavior. When you actively try to control your own life, you are attempting contingency management.

Contingency management tactics require minimal effort but pay off fast and big. In fact, the ease and simplicity of using them puts some people off. "That's just plain common sense," "My mother pulled those tactics," and "Too simple," are some of the reactions of people hearing them for the first time. Yet these tactics have worked for people in curing just about every variety of procrastinating there is.

Tactic 1: Grandma's Rule

Remember when you were a child running out the door to play with friends? A voice often called you back: "Can't leave until you clean up your room!" Your room got cleaned up really fast—then off you went.

This first tactic involves doing to yourself what your parents used to do for you. Before you allow yourself to do something you like, *do one thing you usually put off.* (It also helps if you set a specific time to finish it.) The more pleasant task then becomes your reward.

Examples: You have a habit of letting the dinner dishes pile up. You like to watch television or play Scrabble after dinner. *Don't let yourself watch the tube or play word games until the dishes are done!*

You've been putting off doing a household repair project. You'd like to go out to dinner with friends. Set a date for completing the repairs and make dinner reservations for the following evening. *Don't go unless your project is finished!*

You've been putting off seeing the doctor about your chest pain. You continually forget, or else you're too busy. *Don't do anything until you make an appointment!* (As soon as you make the appointment, get back into your normal routine.)

Tactic 2: Make It Easy to Start

If you'd only begin, you'd find it easy to continue. The trick is to make it easy to take the first step. Arrange whatever you need so that the first step is within arm's reach, right under your nose.

Examples: You've been thinking about taking up a new hobby for months, but you've done absolutely nothing beyond thinking about it. Go to the store for materials, supplies, and necessary equipment. Get the required instructions. With everything you need close at hand, you'll be much more likely to do something with your new interest the next time it comes to mind. *When you think about it, do it!*

You've been putting off writing a report. Clear everything off your desk. Then get together the paper, pens, typing equipment, background information, and references you will need for your report. Lay them out neatly so that when you do have an impulse to get in gear, you'll be off and running. *Take advantage of that impulse!*

Tactic 3:
Schedule, Schedule, Schedule

Many things don't get done because the plans for accomplishing them are too vague. Procrastination couldn't be easier when there is no definite target for completion. Many people find that by simply assigning a deadline for starting or a deadline for completion, they accomplish far more.

Examples: You live in a house where the garbage piles up quickly. Each person in the household means to take a turn, but meanwhile your place is beginning to smell like a stockyard. *Make a schedule for who takes the garbage out when–and stick to it!*

You've been dreaming about a vacation for months. You've got a place in mind, but you've done nothing about it. Meanwhile you've been working so hard that you're getting frazzled. Schedule that vacation trip as part of your work. *Set a target date for your departure and hold to it!*

Tactic 4: Breaking Down Big Projects

Many things are put off because they seem like the rainbow and the pot of gold. What you have to do may look too big or too far off, so you sit around stewing over the enormity of it. The solution is to break the job down into manageable proportions and provide intermediate payoffs along the way.

Examples: Your house is a mountain of disarray from twenty years of collecting junk, odds and ends, and memorabilia. Sorting things out seems an impossible job. Work on the house by rooms or sections, taking them one at a time. At the completion of each room, pat yourself on the back and reward yourself with a break. *Then tackle the next room!*

You want to find a job, but don't know where to start. Divide the project into small tasks that you can handle. Figure out your best sources for getting leads (such as friends, newspapers, trade journals, phone book). Spend some time every day working with these sources. Get together appropriate clothing. Prepare a résumé with your background, social security number, and references. Allow time each day for making the rounds or pounding the pavement. Keep lists of the places you contact. And be sure to congratulate yourself as you accomplish each step.

Tactic 5: Get Others to Help

Other people can help you fight procrastination. Things can get done faster with more brains and hands. And you can stroke each other for making progress. People not directly involved can provide support by prodding you when you slack off. You can *yoke* yourself to others who are willing to cooperate. (Yoking has to do with interrelated commitments. You say "I will do such and such if you will do such and such.")

Examples: The house looks like a hurricane has hit. You are feeling those familiar feelings of reluctance and know that it's just not going to get cleaned up if you try to do it by your lonesome. Get your kids, your friends, or your mate in on the project with you. Divvy up responsibilities. Encourage one another as you work, and make a point of congratulating each other on the progress you make.

You have a big report to do (my favorite example, especially when writing a book). Make your partner, your friends, and your associates aware of your project. Tell them how much you have planned to do each day. *Ask them to stroke you when you do your planned assignment and penalize you if you don't!* You might agree that if you slack off you have to make your own dinner, skip the tennis game, or endure the cold shoulder from your cohorts.

Both you and a friend are putting things off. You are not practicing your clarinet, and your friend is not learning French for his forthcoming trip abroad. *Make a pact detailing that if you practice an hour each day, your friend will study French for an hour!* Report to each other how you are doing. Give one another pep talks if there is any slacking off.

Tactic 6:
Make the Delay Unbearable

Many things get done only when people can't stand putting them off for another minute. The basis of this last tactic is to hasten this process and make it *unbearable* to procrastinate. To do this, put whatever you've been avoiding doing right in front of you (or go to where it's located). Drop everything else. Confront what you've been putting off by concentrating on it. Keep thinking about it and how long you've been delaying doing it. Sooner or later you'll be driven to do it just to get it out of the way.

Examples: You've put off working on the second car for weeks. Now get the tools out. Sit in front of the car and stare at it. Consider all the energy you've devoted to not fixing it. *Don't move or blink until you pick up the wrench and yank something!*

For months you've been putting off a discussion with a family member. Drop all your activities. Stay in the house and think about nothing but how much damage is being done by your delay. Whenever you look at that person, think of what you've been avoiding saying. *Don't do anything that could distract you from getting it out!*

A FEW MORE DOS AND DON'TS

Don't think you are alone! Almost everyone procrastinates, and many do so because of fears. If what slows you down is fear, perhaps a word from a friend or something inspirational from a favorite text might start you moving. However, if procrastination is crippling your life, *do* consider seeking professional guidance.

Do realize that life can be pressured, demanding, and

bewildering. As life becomes more complicated, you may lose the ability to focus your energies, efforts, and interests.

Don't believe, however, that the confusion and feeling of spinning your wheels are necessarily permanent. Learn to set priorities. This will eliminate confusion and put you in control.

Don't think of procrastination as a sin that you have to stamp out in yourself. Procrastination is a natural part of life (you aren't too likely to meet many people who have never procrastinated about anything!)

Even though you can't wipe it out completely, you can use these techniques to reduce your level of procrastination. To expect yourself never to delay anything again is unrealistic. A time clock never procrastinates. But you aren't a time clock and neither am I. Perhaps any one of these suggestions is all you'll need to get the job done. Or maybe you will choose to use several of these tactics at the same time. The key is *to use them and stick to them.* You'll then begin to lose the habit of putting things off. The rapid improvement in your productivity, apparent will power, and determination will amaze you and the people around you.

INTRODUCING
THE SERIES EDITOR:
DONALD M. DIBLE

Don Dible presents more than 100 speeches, seminars and workshops a year all across the United States under the sponsorship of universities, trade associations, chambers of commerce, business magazines, professional societies, and private companies.

His lucid, enthusiastic, experience-backed presentations are designed to inspire and motivate seminar participants and convention audiences to put to immediate use the highly-practical information he covers.

In preparing his talks, Don draws from a rich and varied background. He received his BSEE from MIT and his MSEE from Stanford University. Prior to launching his first business in 1971, he served in engineering and sales management capacities with three companies, including a subsidiary of the SCM Corporation, where he was responsible for directing and training a large national sales organization producing millions of dollars in sales annually.

In seven years Don founded eight successful businesses in the publishing, advertising, seminar, graphic arts services, and real estate industries. All but one of these companies was started on a part-time basis with modest capital resources. Each of Mr. Dible's businesses reflect the unusual and innovative approach he takes to sales, marketing and finance—topics discussed in detail during his many seminars and talks.

While Don is still blazing new trails in his speaking career, he is perhaps best known for his work in the field of publishing.

Prior to writing his 100,000-copy bestseller, *Up Your OWN Organization!,* Don had never written a single word for publication in his life. Aside from writing themes, book reports, and term papers in high school and college, his only major writing project was a highly technical undergraduate thesis at the Massachusetts Institute of Technology.

After working for seven years in industry, Don became frustrated with the rigidly structured world of big business. He looked longingly and lovingly at the outside world of entrepreneurship—and decided to launch his own business.

Following three years of research, including attendance at numerous seminars, interviews with hundreds of successful small business owner/managers, and a thorough review of the small-business books in print at the time, (mostly dry-as-a-bone textbooks and rah-rah get-rich-quick books), he finally decided that the most needed new product in the marketplace was a *realistic* book about starting a new business. Faithful to his commitment, he raised the needed capital; and with the assistance of his dedicated wife he started The Entrepreneur Press. Next he hired a secretary, and in just four months produced a 750-page manuscript for *Up Your OWN Organization!,* with an Introduction by Robert Townsend, former Chairman of the

Board of Avis Rent-a-Car and bestselling author of *Up The Organization.*

Shortly after the publication of his first book, Don was asked to assist a professional society in organizing and presenting a two-day conference utilizing the services of fourteen attorneys, accountants, business consultants and financial executives. The program was recorded, the recordings were transcribed, and he edited and adapted the transcripts into manuscript form. The resulting book was *How to Plan and Finance a Growing Business.*

As a result of the success of The Entrepreneur Press, Don has published the following books: *Up Your OWN Organization!; How to Plan and Finance a Growing Business; Small Business Success Secrets: How to Zap the Competition and Zoom Your Profits With Smart Marketing; How to Make Money in Your Own Small Business; Fundamentals of Record-Keeping and Finance for the Small Business; What Everybody Should Know about Patents, Trademarks and Copyrights; Business Startup Basics; Techniques and Strategies for Effective Small Business Management; Profitable Advertising Techniques for Small Businesses;* and *How to Make a Fortune in Import/Export.*

Recently Don founded a new publishing enterprise, the Showcase Publishing Company, dedicated to multi-author motivational and inspirational self-help books. This is the eighth volume published by this company.

Finally, Don has been a guest on scores of television and radio talk shows, including NBC's *Monitor,* with Bill Cullen, and ABC's award-winning *Mike Wallace at Large.* He is also a frequent contributor to magazines such as *Dun's Review, Success Unlimited,* MBA *Magazine, Free Enterprise,* and *Boardroom Reports.*

You may contact Don by writing to him at 3422 Astoria Circle, Fairfield, CA 94533; or by telephoning (707) 422-6822.

235

This book was designed & produced
by George Mattingly, at GM Design, Berkeley
from Trump Mediaeval & Friz Quadrata types
set by Robert Sibley, Abracadabra, San Francisco
and was printed & bound by R. R. Donnelley & Sons
Crawfordsville, Indiana.